Spiritual KNEADING

THROUGH *the* JEWISH MONTHS

BUILDING *the* SACRED *through* CHALLAH

DAHLIA ABRAHAM-KLEIN

TABLE OF CONTENTS

MONTHS OF THE JEWISH YEAR

Additional Challah Recipes

Additional Challah Shapes

Dedicated to my beloved father, of blessed memory

Yehuda Abraham

Just as he touched the lives of thousands of Jews all around the world
may his work continue to inspire world Jewry through this book and me.

Spiritual Kneading Through the Jewish Months:
Building the Sacred through Challah
by Dahlia Abraham-Klein

Cover and Interior Design: Joanna Dion Brown Graphic Design
Publisher: Shamashi Press
Editor: Deborah Megnagni Bailey
Library of Congress Catalog Number: 2014919281
ISBN: 978-0-692-29567-0
1. Cooking: Regional & Ethnic, Jewish 2. Religion: Holidays, Jewish 3. Religion: Judaism, Kabbalah & Mystiscism.
First Edition
10 9 8 7 6 5 4 3 2 1
Printed in the United States

Foreword

In 1971, Dennis Gabor (Günszberg), a scientist whose Jewish family fled from the Nazis in the 1930s, was awarded the Nobel Prize in Physics for his invention of holography, a technique for creating 3-D photographs. One of the unusual aspects of a holographic photo, called a hologram, can be seen when it is broken into small pieces: each piece of the hologram contains the whole image. It seems impossible, but it is true.

The great Jewish Sages explain a similar notion regarding the *mitzvot* (positive commandments).

A wise and clever rabbi was once asked by a Jew with no Jewish education how to enter Jewish tradition. The student complained that the tradition was so vast. Where does one even start?

The rabbi offered a down-to-earth, practical response. But the response also had a secret embedded within it.

"Pick just one *mitzvah*," the rabbi advised, "but pick one you feel you can do forever. If you don't feel you can commit your lifetime to certain *mitzvot*, don't start with any of them. Pick one you are confident you can do for the rest of your life."

The rabbi added, "And then become an expert on that one *mitzvah*. Find out everything you can about it. Study it. Learn it. In all of its detail. Just that one *mitzvah*. Become the world's authority."

The secret, of course, is this: each *mitzvah* contains all of the others. By exploring the depths of one *mitzvah*, you are led to a profound, uplifting entanglement with all of the *mitzvot*.

Spiritual Kneading through the Jewish Months: Building the Sacred through Challah is an exquisite example of precisely this phenomenon. Through an in-depth, beautifully written, thoroughly researched exploration of challah, this book, guided by its gifted author, transforms itself into a gateway into all of Jewish tradition.

Readers of this remarkable book will return to it again and again. From the most practical advice and insights to the most meaningful spiritual Truths, this is not a book about challah; it is a holy sefer concerning our relationship with the Almighty.

One could say this book is truly a challah-gram.

Arthur Kurzweil
author of the classic best seller
From Generation to Generation,
Kabbalah for Dummies
and *The Torah for Dummies*

Introduction

THE FEMININE DIMENSION
OF ROSH CHODESH AND CHALLAH

The First Mitzvah[1]

Immediately prior to the exodus from Egypt, God gave the Israelites their very first *mitzvah* as a people: to mark — and sanctify — the months of the year. As they were leaving darkness and heading toward renewal, the people were given the moon's monthly renewal as a model to follow and emulate: "The renewal of the moon shall be unto you the festival of the head of the month, it shall be unto you the first of the months of the year."[2] The new moon is an emblem of renewal and hope: even as the moon is renewed through natural law, so too the newly-freed people would always possess the potential to renew themselves through their own free will.

Most calendars in use throughout the world are solar-based, marking the 365-day rotation of the earth around the sun. In accordance with the *mitzvah* of Rosh Chodesh, the Jewish calendar is primarily lunar-based, with its months calculated via the phases of the moon, although its year is solar. The twelve lunar months add up to a 354-day year. To make up the eleven missing days and keep the solar and lunar aspects of the year in synch, an additional 'leap' month is added every two or three years. This additional month is called Adar *Bet* (a second Adar).

In ancient times, the sighting of the new moon was cause for grand festivity alongside great seriousness. The phases of the moon define the structure of the Jewish calendar. Every Jewish community was obligated to observe holidays at the right time, and dates were determined based on the sighting of the new moon.

---

1 In common usage, a *mitzvah* often means a good deed or commandment. While this is certainly correct, the word *mitzvah* is related to the Aramaic word tzavta, (Talmud, Bava Metzia 28a) meaning "connection." Thereby, a *mitzvah* can be seen as a conduit connecting God and man, and earth to heaven. Doing *mitzvot* strengthens the bond between man and God while refraining from misdeeds, such as lying and stealing, prevents a breakdown of that bond.

2 Exodus 12:2

During the Second Temple period (530 BCE to 70 CE), the new month was declared when at least two reputable witnesses saw the first sliver of the new moon. The witnesses were called before the Sanhedrin (the rabbinic court) of Jerusalem, and the judges would interview each witness separately to hear their testimonies about the precise location and appearance of the moon. If they gave identical testimonies, the Sanhedrin would declare the arrival of *Rosh Chodesh* — the 'head', i.e. the first day, of the new month. Sacrifices were offered and incense was burnt. Special prayers were chanted, the shofar was blown, and a celebratory meal was eaten. The news of the moon's appearance was communicated to Jewish communities throughout the Land of Israel and the Diaspora via fires lit on hilltops; the first fires lit in Jerusalem would be seen by neighboring communities, who would then light their own fires, and so it would continue, with the news of the new moon passing from hilltop to hilltop.

Toward the end of the Second Temple period, the practice changed: rather than lighting fires, the Sanhedrin began sending messengers to outlying towns and villages to alert them of the appearance of the moon. This was due to the fact that the Samaritans[3] had begun to set fires at incorrect times in order to deliberately mislead the Jews. By the middle of the fourth century, when oppression and persecution by the Romans threatened the continued existence of the Sanhedrin, Hillel the Nasi[4] took the extraordinary step of establishing a fixed calendar. He made public the system of calendar calculation, which up to then had been a closely guarded secret. Thereafter, the sending out of messengers to proclaim the new moon was discontinued.

Today we still follow the fixed calendar, although tradition dictates that every month the new moon is proclaimed in synagogue on the Shabbat preceding its appearance. (This Shabbat is known as *Shabbat Mevarchim* — the Shabbat of Blessing [the new moon].) At the end of the morning service, when the Torah reading has been completed, the Torah is raised for all to see, and the rabbi announces when the new moon will be 'born,' giving the exact date and time. A new moon is born at the moment when the moon is completely hidden between the sun and the earth; six hours after this '*molad*,' or birth, a crescent of light reflects off the moon, making it visible. The rabbi is quite specific about the time of the *molad*, down to the exact *chelek*.[5] Next, the leader of the service recites a prayer for the new month, *Birkat Hachodesh*. As part of that prayer, he informs the congregation exactly when Rosh Chodesh will fall — whether it will last for one or two days, and on which day(s) of the week.[6]

---

3   The Samaritans were an Abrahamic religion closely related to Judaism. Its adherents claimed that they were the true Israel, descendants of the "lost" tribes taken into Assyrian captivity. They had their own temple on Mount Gerizim and claimed that it was the original sanctuary. Moreover, they claimed that their version of the Holy Books of Moses was the original, and that the Jews had a falsified text produced during the Babylonian exile.

4   Hillel the Nasi was the head of the Sanhedrin at that time.

5   Chelek literally means portion; in this situation it refers to portions of a minute. The lunar cycle is 29 days, 12 hours, and 793 chalakim, and each chelek is equal to 3 and 1/3 seconds.

6   When the preceding month is thirty days, Rosh Chodesh is observed for two days (the thirtieth day of the previous month and the first day of the new month), and when the preceding month is twenty-nine days, Rosh Chodesh is observed for only one day (the first day of the new month).

On Rosh Chodesh itself, prayers are added to the synagogue service. The additional service (*Musaf*) that is recited on every Shabbat and Festival is added, as is *Hallel*, and there is a special Torah reading. Finally, *Kiddush Levanah,* the ceremony of the sanctification of the New Moon, takes place outdoors on a clear night soon after Rosh Chodesh, customarily on the first Saturday night of the month. We observe Rosh Chodesh eleven times a year, excepting only Rosh Hashanah, because the festival of the New Year incorporates the new month.

In its essence, Rosh Chodesh is about renewal; that first tiny, luminous sliver of light that heralds the beginning of a fresh new cycle. Rosh Chodesh literally means *Head of the Month*. In human terms, your head, your *rosh*, contains the spark of innovation that will be made manifest through your body's actions. The crescent moon of Rosh Chodesh is about potential rather than actualization, about reaching for greatness and having faith that it will develop in due course. We, too, have the power to start over, and it starts with the *rosh*. We can work on ourselves as the moon is waxing, and change course, if necessary, before the full moon arrives. Through our actions we can become 'full,' illuminating the world with our deeds.

Women and Rosh Chodesh

Rosh Chodesh holds a special significance for women, and is considered a mini-holiday. The holiday was given specifically to Jewish women as a reward for not having been willing to participate in the sin of the Golden Calf. When the Israelites were in the Sinai desert, Moses went up Mount Sinai in order to receive the Torah from God. After he had been gone for forty days, the Israelites left waiting for him at the foot of the mountain began to fear that he was dead. In their fear, the Israelite men beseeched Aaron, Moses' brother, to make them a golden calf, an idol to worship in place of God, who they thought had abandoned them.

In order to fulfill their wish, Aaron told the men that he would need the jewelry belonging to their families: "And Aaron said: Take the earrings from your wives, sons and daughters, and bring them to me."[7] According to a *midrash* (rabbinic legend)[8] based on this verse, the women refused to give their jewelry to their husbands, who ultimately had to wrench it away from them. Although life in the desert without Moses to lead them seemed threatening and hopeless, the Israelite women kept faith with him, certain that he would return as he had promised. In these dark moments they let their inner light guide them forward, willing to believe in the power of renewal and to trust God no matter how difficult things seemed. The moon wanes into darkness but then returns, growing brighter and bigger until it fills the sky with its light; darkness, both physical and spiritual, is banished. The women were given a reward for their faith; although Rosh Chodesh

---

7   Exodus 32:2

8   There are two types of midrash: midrash aggada and midrash halacha. Midrash aggada can best be described as a form of storytelling that explores ethics and values in biblical texts. Whereas midrash aggada focuses on biblical characters as they pertain to values and ideas, midrash halacha focuses on Jewish law and practice. Midrash halacha attempts to take biblical texts that are either general or unclear and to clarify what they mean.

is marked by all Jews, Jewish women were given a special part in its observance — they are supposed to abstain from work, and engage in a day of pampering.

Since the rise of modern feminism in the 1960s, there has been an upsurge of Rosh Chodesh groups all over the world aimed at gathering women together to celebrate Rosh Chodesh. There is no one way to mark the day; every group chooses its own path, whether it be through grappling with Jewish texts, discussing issues that pertain to Jewish women, or simply having a women-only gathering.

Separating Challah

How does this special celebration of Rosh Chodesh by women connect with the baking of challah? The beginnings of an answer can be found in another midrashic verse, which states: "One who fulfills the *mitzvah* of *hafrashat challah* (separating challah), it is as if he nullified the worship of idols, while one who does not fulfill the *mitzvah* of separating challah, it's as if he sustains the worship of idols."[9] What does this mean?

When the people of Israel were in the desert, they were instructed in the many commandments they would be required to fulfill once they entered the Promised Land. One such commandment was the giving of a dough offering: "The Lord spoke to Moses saying: Speak to the children of Israel and you shall say to them, When you arrive in the Land to which I am bringing you, and you eat from the bread of the Land, you shall set aside a gift for the Lord. The first portion of your dough, you shall separate a loaf for a gift; as in the case of the gift of the threshing floor, so shall you separate it. From the first portion of your dough you shall give a gift to the Lord in [all] your generations."[10]

During biblical times, these verses were the source of the system of tithing bread. The *Kohanim* — priests — did not own or work land; the rest of the people gave them tithes from their own produce so that they could be sustained while fulfilling their priestly tasks. Every time bread was made, a part of the dough was separated to be baked for the priests. This part was called '*challah*' and the term now also refers to the loaves we eat today.

The destruction of the Temple meant the cessation of tithing; it became transmuted into the current practice of *hafrashat challah*, in which a portion of challah is still taken and separated, but instead of being given to *kohanim*, it is burned and rendered inedible, commemorating this interdependence between the Israelites and the *kohanim*.

---

9 Vayikra Rabbah 15:6.

10 Numbers 15:17-21

There is a famous verse in the Torah that states: "Make Me a *Mikdash* (sanctuary) and I will dwell among them."[11] The Sages point out that the verse does not say "in it," but rather, "among them,"[12] which they interpret to mean that if you make space for it, then the Divine Presence can and will dwell within each Jew. By extension, every Jewish home has the potential to be a microcosm of the Sanctuary, and the various labors that we perform within our homes are comparable to those of a *kohen* working in the Holy Temple. It may seem that the *kohen* was doing work of a purely material nature, but in actuality all of his tasks were carried out with the intention of fulfilling the will of God; so can it be in our homes.

Today, any cook at home must take and separate challah when they use more than fifty-nine ounces (1.6 kg) of wheat, rye, barley, oat or spelt flour. The liquid mixed with the flour should be mostly water. After the dough is kneaded, but before it is shaped into loaves, it is all placed into a single bowl and a blessing is recited: "Blessed are you, Lord our God, King of the Universe, who has sanctified us with His commandments and commanded us to separate the challah."[13] Then a small piece of the dough is taken — approximately an ounce (27 g) — and the baker declares, "This is challah." Lastly the challah is wrapped in foil and burned under a broiler or in the oven.

There are many preliminary steps that have taken place before that piece of dough is separated in the comfort of our kitchens. Soil must be plowed, the grains must be planted, then watered, the crops must be reaped, the kernels must be sifted… the list goes on and on. After investing all that time and effort, a farmer may come to the mistaken conclusion that it was his great exertion, with the help of "Mother Nature," that led to his harvest. Likewise, a baker may come to think that the bread they have produced is solely the result of their efforts. It is easy to fall into a trap where we believe that the more we work, the more we earn, and that our earnings are based on our efforts alone. But this attitude actually borders on idol worship, because idol worship is the belief in an independent self outside of God. It is the worship of self-honor and self-aggrandizement rather than of a greater being — the Almighty who really bestows upon us our bread, through his loving-kindness.

This is where the *mitzvah* of separating challah comes in, and why the *Midrash* claims that one who fulfills the *mitzvah* is nullifying idol worship. The ingredients have been mixed together skillfully by stretching, pushing and pulling the dough. During this physical workout, the woman of the home pauses for an introspective moment, separates a portion of the dough and says a blessing. She then lifts it up and says, "This is challah." This conscious act signifies the woman's recognition that the dough, that most basic staple of the human diet, is not simply a result of human effort, but is a gift from God. By extension, she is recognizing that the same is true of all our material successes in life. We, like the *kohanim*, depend on God for physical sustenance in order to perform our mission in life.

---

11 Exodus 25:8

12 Talmud (Megillah 29a): God will dwell in the holy spaces we create, for they are the Temple in miniature.

13 If you use more than forty-three ounces but less than fifty-nine, you separate the challah but do not recite the blessing.

Making challah is one of the special *mitzvot* entrusted to women, although a man may bake it if there is no woman in the home, or when the woman grants him permission to perform the *mitzvah*. The first time baking bread is referred to in the Torah is with our foremother, Sarah. When the angels came to visit Abraham, he went to prepare the meal for them himself, however the making of bread he left to his wife: "Abraham rushed to Sarah's tent, and he said, 'Quickly, get three *se'ah* of sifted flour, knead them and make loaves.'"[14] The Talmud tells us that Sarah's bread stayed fresh from Friday to Friday and a cloud (the *Shechina,* known as the feminine dimension of God's divine presence) hovered over her tent,[15] and when she died, these miracles ceased. These miracles anticipated the current reality; that it would be the woman who would eventually have the special *mitzvah* of *hafrashat challah*, and through it, the capacity to bring the *Shechina* into her dwelling. Sarah left an indelible imprint on each of us to inspire us to emulate her greatness.

Spiritual Kneading

In the sanctuary of our homes, we are graced with a special capacity to meditate and to converse with God while kneading dough. Love and faith is infused into the challah, which then serves as both physical and spiritual sustenance for our families. We are the bread winners!

When we knead dough properly, we feel it in our arms. We shape the dough, we push and pull it, we flip it upside down; we work with it until it yields to us and becomes elastic. There aren't many other foods we make that require us to work so hard. Beyond the physical effort involved, manually kneading the dough connects us to a tradition of our ancestors that has been practiced for thousands of years, before modern appliances made our lives both easier and infinitely more complicated. It is a reminder that the choice to move at our own pace in the modern world is a conscious one, and that sometimes slowing down is best for our mental health and clarity.

To be fully mindful of what we are doing, we must meditate to the tempo of the knead. Although there is a common belief that meditation is an Eastern art, in fact Judaism has also historically used different forms of meditation. An early example in the Torah is when our patriarch Isaac is described as going to *"lasuach"*[16] in the field — a term understood by all commentators as some type of meditative practice.[17]

Although the topic of meditation is far too grand for the scope of this book, in the most general sense, meditation is thinking, using your *rosh* in a controlled manner for a period of time with a specific *kavanah*, intention, and then actualizing that intention. As Jews, we can actualize our *kavanah* through *mitzvot*. This

---

14 Genesis 18:6

15 Genesis Rabbah 60:16

16 Genesis 24:63

17 Kaplan, Aryeh. (1978), Meditation and the Bible, Maine, Samuel Weiser Inc, p.101

book features a different guided intention each month to be focused on while kneading the dough, as a way to elevate the action and bring us closer to God.

The first step to having the right *kavanah* is through practicing breath control. When God created Adam, the Torah says, "God formed man out of the dust of the ground, and breathed into his nostrils a breath of life. Man [thus] became a living creature."[18] The Hebrew word for breath is *neshima*, while the Hebrew word for soul is *neshama*. We can understand from this verse that breath and soul are intimately connected. God breathed into man and by doing so, bestowed upon him a spark of the divine — a soul. God did not breathe into any other creature but Adam. Only man has the ability to use his breath in order to control his mind, and by doing so, draw closer to God.

Although there are many modalities in meditation, in this book each monthly meditation will always start with repeated controlled breathing. It is important to repeat a practice to habituate the mind to it. Learning to breathe in a controlled manner trains us to breathe from the diaphragm, slowly and consciously, in a more mindful way.

You may have noticed that when a person is praying they have a tendency to sway back and forth, or side to side. In most cases, this is done quite unconsciously; the soul is responding to the natural rhythm of the prayer. The prayer (action) elevates the soul, and that elevation is expressed bodily through swaying, synching with the prayers. This swaying motion is a form of meditation, and it can be translated into the kneading of the dough. The action of kneading backwards and forwards, using controlled breath and *kavanah*, becomes the physical vehicle to spiritually elevate the dough.

First of the Month, First of the Dough

Just as Rosh Chodesh marks the first of the month, so too, challah is referred to in the Torah as *reishit* — "the first" because it was the first of the dough that had to be separated to be given to the *Kohanim*. In the *midrash* it says that God created the world in the merit of the *mitzvot* that are referred to as *reishit* — another fascinating connection between the two *mitzvot*.[19] We are required to mark Rosh Chodesh in order to organize our lives and know when the festivals fall. Knowing when to do what means that we can fulfill *mitzvot* appropriately. Likewise, the most basic aspect of fulfilling our daily need for sustenance — baking bread — *first* requires that we demonstrate our appreciation to God for giving us that sustenance.

---

18 Genesis 2:7

19 Bereishit Rabbah 1:4

There is another *midrashic* text that refers to Adam, the first man, as the "challah of the world,"[20] because of the manner in which he was created — God gathered dust and mixed it with water, creating a clay similar to dough.[21] Interestingly, within the word challah is the word *chol*, sand, one of the lowest elements of creation. I like to see that as a hint that separating the challah is one of the most important *mitzvot* we do, reflecting our primary mission in life: interacting with the material world for the purpose of elevating it, and through that, connecting with the Source from which it came.

---

20 Bereishit Rabbah on Genesis 2:21

21 Genesis 2:6: "And a mist ascended from the earth and watered the entire surface of the ground." Rashi explains that God brought up the [waters of the] deep and watered the clouds to soak the earth, and man was created; like the baker, who puts water [into the flour] and afterwards kneads the dough. Here too, "He watered," and afterwards, "He formed" [man]. — [from Exodus Rabbah 30:113; Pirkei d'Rabbi Eliezer, ch. 5]

With Rosh Chodesh traditionally being a woman's holiday, it is a natural time for women to gather together and be active participants in their heritage. Members of a Rosh Chodesh Challah Baking group following this book will become "Spiritual Kneaders," enhancing their spiritual growth via the tradition of challah baking, while meditating upon the Jewish theme of the month. Chatting, kneading, meditating and Torah study: women united in a wave of baking and braiding throughout the world.

This book does not have to be restricted to use only within the context of a Rosh Chodesh group, of course; it can also be used simply as a challah cookbook that offers creative ways to bring spirituality to your Shabbat table. It can be used as a course of study for girls as they prepare for their *Bat Mitzvah*, or for the bride-to-be preparing to carry forth the tradition of her foremothers into her new home — a new bride can set the tone and aura in her home with meaningful challah baking. There is an extra chapter on the tradition of baking challah in a cohort of forty women as a *segulah* in someone's merit, be it for them to have an easy childbirth, to find a soul mate, or to recover from illness. These are further opportunities for women to gather for a sacred event with a common intention.

The book covers all thirteen months of the Jewish year, including the leap month of *Adar Bet*, with a specific curriculum of study for each month. In addition, there is an introductory chapter for a group meeting that covers everything you need to know about challah. After following the *Spiritual Kneading* process for a year, this book can also be used as a blueprint for starting another cycle of *Spiritual Kneading*, with the help of **Further Reading** suggestions at the back of the book.

The syllabus for each month opens with a specific challah recipe and shape, although you are also welcome to create your own individual designs, or choose from a recipe or shape found in the **Appendices**. There are optional Rosh Chodesh psalms to be read at the beginning of the meeting to welcome the new month. Next follows an explanation of the theme of the month, specifically as it connects with baking challah and the symbolic character of the ingredients. A point-by-point month-specific meditation guide follows, for use during the kneading of the challah. Finally, you will find additional material that builds on the theme that was introduced at the beginning of the chapter, presenting further ideas and questions to be discussed by the group while the challah is rising. The purpose of baking challah in this particular way is to develop your own personal spiritual growth within the context of a Rosh Chodesh group.

According to *The Book of Formation*, the earliest kabbalistic text, each Jewish month has a corresponding color (Sefer Yetzirah 4:14). One who wishes to energize the influence within that month has to contemplate, or clothe himself/herself in, the particular color. To represent this, I have used the color of each month for the corresponding chapter title and subheadings, to highlight its governing influence.[22]

The Torah themes and texts explored in *Spiritual Kneading through the Jewish Months* are relevant to all Jews, no matter which denomination they are affiliated with — and indeed, even if they are totally unaffiliated.

Spiritual Kneading through the Jewish Months Planner

The following is a guideline of general suggestions on how to get the group off the ground.

The first meeting

If you have created a new group for *Spiritual Kneading*, and the women do not know each other yet, then when you first meet you will need time for introductions and becoming familiar with each other. Creativity can only be unleashed fully in a comfortable place. Even if you are already friends, there may be things you do not know about each other that would be appropriate to share before you embark on this spiritually conscious journey together. You can start with everyone giving their Hebrew names and what they mean. Jewish calendars should be distributed to each member of the group as a guide for the months to come, so that those who are unfamiliar with the Jewish yearly cycle will be prepared. You can always find Jewish calendars at the local Chabad house, any local synagogue or even at kosher supermarkets. They are all usually only too happy to give them out for free.

Ask those present to share their expectations for the group. Have someone record these ideas, to be explored in future meetings. Before the initial *Spiritual Kneading*, members need to contribute all the necessary equipment needed for challah baking, a list of which is found below, and to have extra copies of this book for the group to follow along. Set a date and place for the next gathering. This is where each woman having a calendar becomes very useful, as you can all make sure you are available on the right days — the New Moon does not fall on the same day every month.

I suggest assigning a host and co-host, and that they become the coordinators and guides for the following month, and that the hosts change monthly. The hosts will plan the event and familiarize themselves with the text, so that they can guide the group through the material. However during the **Discussion during the Rising**, the entire group will study the text together, discuss reflective questions, and for some months, follow specific exercises. At the time of ***hafrashat challah***, the hosts will once again step up as group leaders, guiding the group throughout the remainder of the meeting.

---

22 BaMidbar Rabbah 2:7 has a list of each of the twelve tribes of Israel and its corresponding flag, color, stone, and symbol associated with it. The color of each flag was like the twelve colors of the precious stones that were over the heart (breastplate) of Aaron, the High Priest. From this the kingdoms learned to make flags and a color for each flag. The Zohar correlates the twelve signs of the zodiac to the twelve Hebrew months and the twelve tribes of Israel (I:173).

The monthly meeting will follow this outline

1. Optional Rosh Chodesh Psalms are recited.
2. Introduction to Challah Theme during the Yeast Activation — discover symbolic importance of each ingredient as it relates to the challah theme of the month
3. Meditation during the kneading — everyone may take turns kneading if there is one bowl within the group
4. Discussion during the Rising (one hour) — Jewish text is studied and reflected upon
5. *Kavanah* (intention) for *hafrashat challah* — a focused thought before the blessing
6. *Hafrashat challah* (separation of the dough) — blessing is recited (given on page 17)
7. Shaping the Dough
8. Baking is done at home

The equipment that you will need for the challah baking

Large bowl with a wide mouth
Spatula
Bench knife
Rolling pin
Measuring cups
Measuring spoons
Flour sifter
Egg brush
Small bowls (for the eggs)

The equipment will move, month to month, with the coordinator of the month. Every month, the recipe changes. To cultivate inclusivity, I suggest that you ask each participant to bring an ingredient to the *Spiritual Kneading* group; in this way everyone integrates and weaves a part of themselves into the collective *mitzvah* of celebrating Rosh Chodesh and baking challah. If participants want to bring their own equipment to make their own batch of dough, this should be encouraged as well — the goal is to make challah and for women to be united in a fun and meaningful activity. The duration of each meeting will be approximately two hours and thirty minutes (the actual baking of the challah is done afterward, in the participants' homes).

Calendar at a glance

Your first gathering should be about learning the fundamental *mitzvah* of challah as explained in the chapter, *What You Knead to Know about Challah*. Thereafter, continue on the Rosh Chodesh of the following month. The first month of the year is Tishrei; traditionally, the world was created on the first of Tishrei. However, the exodus from Egypt took place in the month of Nissan, signaling the birth of the Jewish nation, therefore Nissan is seen as the first month with regard to national festivals. The **Contents** page lists the different monthly themes you will cover.

Separating Challah

PROCEDURE AND BLESSING

Hafrashat Challah

> *"The Lord spoke to Moses saying: Speak to the children of Israel and you shall say to them, When you arrive in the Land to which I am bringing you, and you eat from the bread of the Land, you shall set aside a gift for the Lord. The first portion of your dough, you shall separate a loaf for a gift; as in the case of the gift of the threshing floor, so shall you separate it. From the first portion of your dough you shall give a gift to the Lord in [all] your generations."*
>
> (Numbers 15:17-21)

We call the loaves we eat on Shabbat and festivals "challah" because that was the term used to describe the portion of dough that was separated during Temple times to be given to the *kohanim*. The *kohanim* were deeply involved in their service in the Temple, and did not possess their own land to farm, and were therefore unable to fully provide for their families. God commanded us to give His portion — His challah — to the *kohanim* as a means of sustenance for them. Since we no longer have the Temple, we may not give this portion to a *kohen*, nor eat it ourselves. Still, we continue to be obligated in our observance of the *mitzvah* of *hafrashat challah*, immortalizing the interdependence between the people and the priests. Nowadays, when we separate this portion of the challah dough, we burn it and dispose of it in an honorable way.

Type of Flour: The commandment applies to any dough (whether used for challah or bread) made from one of the five main species of grain: wheat, barley, oats, rye and spelt.

Liquid: For the commandment to apply, the majority of the liquid content of the dough must be one of the following: water, wine, milk, bee honey or olive oil.

Quantities: The amount of dough that is taken and burned should be a "*kezayit*," a Talmudic measure that literally means "like an olive," and in practice should weigh approximately one ounce, or 27 grams.

Whether you separate challah at all depends on how much flour you are using in your baking. If you are using less than forty-three ounces of flour (about 1 kg), the commandment to separate challah does not apply. If you are using between forty-three and fifty-nine ounces (1.1 kg to 1.6 kg), you separate the challah, but do not make a blessing. If you are using fifty-nine ounces or more flour, you separate the challah and make the blessing.

14

By lifting up a dough-offering to God we are directing our physical needs and urges to a spiritual purpose. The dough takes on a new "life," consecrated for holiness, directed and hallowed for a greater purpose. We are accomplishing a merger of the physical with the spiritual. The *mitzvah* of challah is one of many within Judaism to demonstrate that God is not confined to the realm of spirit alone. *Mitzvot* involving physical activities make Godliness the focal point of our lives.

The letters of the term *"hafrashat challah"* form an acronym that encompasses all the blessings that a woman can bring into her home through the performance of this special *mitzvah*.[23] As it states in Ezekiel, "You shall give the first yield of your dough to the *kohen* to make a blessing rest upon your home" (44:30). When you say the blessing, be mindful that you are beseeching God for all of these divine favors to reside in your dwelling.

ה	*H (Hey)*	*Hatzlacha* — Success
פ	*F (Phei)*	*Parnassah* — Livelihood
ר	*R (Reish)*	*Refuah Sheleima* — Speedy and Full Recovery from Illness
ש	*S (Shin)*	*Shalom Bayit* — Peace in the Home
ת	*T (Taf)*	*Tefillah* — Our Prayers should be Accepted
ח	*C (Chet)*	*Chuppah* — Marriage
ל	*L (Lamed)*	*Leyda Kala* — Easy Birth
ה	*H (Hey)*	*Hod* — Majesty for God

How to Separate Challah

It is customary to stand during this ceremony. Place the dough in front of you, after kneading, but before it has been formed into any sort of shape.

Before fulfilling the *mitzvah* of *hafrashat challah*, some have the custom to give charity, or to perform *netilat yadayim* — ritual hand washing — although this must be done without the usual blessing.[24]

---

23 There are no vowels in the Hebrew alphabet, so the letters referred to here are only the consonants.

24 Although netilat yadayim is traditionally translated as hand washing, its literal meaning is actually raising the hands. The washing or raising of our hands reflects and represents our intention to offer up the deeds of our hands in service to God.

Fill a large cup with water. Pass the cup to your non-dominant hand and pour three times over the other hand. Repeat with the dominant hand.

Prayer for Loved Ones

This is seen as an auspicious time to pray for family and loved ones, and to make personal requests. You may, of course, offer a personal prayer in your own words, or you can recite the following:

יְהִי רָצוֹן מִלְפָנֶיךָ ה' אֱלֹהֵינוּ וֵאלֹהֵי אֲבוֹתֵינוּ שֶׁתְּבָרֵךְ עִסָתֵנוּ כְּמוֹ שֶׁשָׁלַחְתָּ:
בְּרָכָה בְּעִסוֹת אִמוֹתֵינוּ שָׂרָה, רִבְקָה, רָחֵל וְלֵאָה, וִיקַיַם בָּנוּ הַפָּסוּק
"וְרֵאשִׁית עֲרִיסוֹתֵיכֶם תִּתְּנוּ לַכֹּהֵן לְהַנִּיחַ בְּרָכָה אֶל בֵּיתֶךָ"

Transliteration

Yehi ratzon milfanecha Adonai eloheinu v'elohei avoteinu she'tvarech asateinu kmo she-shalachta berachah be'asot imoteinu Sarah, Rivkah, Rachel ve'Leah, veyakim banu hapasuk: "Vereishit arisoteichem titnu lakohen lehaniach berachah el beitecha."

Translation

May it be Your will, our God, the God of our Fathers, that You bless our dough, as You blessed the dough of our Mothers, Sarah, Rivkah, Rachel and Leah. And may we be blessed, as in the verse: "You shall give the first yield of your dough to the kohen to make a blessing rest upon your home." *(Verse from Ezekiel 44:30)*

Prayer for Divine Presence

Some have the custom of reciting the following verse twice before reciting the blessing for separating challah:

וִיהִי נֹעַם אֲדֹנָי אֱלֹהֵינוּ עָלֵינוּ וּמַעֲשֵׂה יָדֵינוּ כּוֹנְנָה עָלֵינוּ וּמַעֲשֵׂה יָדֵינוּ כּוֹנְנֵהוּ

Transliteration

Vayehi noam Adonai eloheinu aleinu u-ma'aseh yadeinu konena aleinu u-ma'aseh yadeinu konenehu

Translation

May the pleasantness of the Lord our God be upon us; establish for us the work of our hands; let the work of our hands prosper. *(Psalms 90:17)*

Separating the Challah

The blessing on separating the dough is slightly different for Ashkenazim and Sephardim. Place your right hand on the dough,[25] without pinching any off, and recite the blessing.

בָּרוּךְ אַתָּה ה' אֱלֹהֵינוּ מֶלֶךְ הָעוֹלָם אֲשֶׁר קִדְּשָׁנוּ בְּמִצְוֹתָיו וְצִוָּנוּ לְהַפְרִישׁ *[חַלָּה *[תְּרוּמָה].

Sephardim

Transliteration

Baruch ata adonai eloheinu melech ha'olam asher kid'shanu bemitzvotav vetzivanu lehafrish challah [terumah].

Translation

Blessed are you, Lord our God, King of the Universe, who has sanctified us with His commandments, and commanded us to separate challah [terumah].

---

25 If you are left-handed, use your left hand.

Remove a small piece of dough, approximately the size of a ping-pong ball, lift it up, and say:

הֲרֵי זוֹ חַלָּה

Transliteration: Harei zo challah
Translation: This is Challah

After this declaration, the custom is to say the following prayer:

יְהִי רָצוֹן מִלְּפָנֶיךָ ה׳ אֱלֹהֵינוּ וֵאלֹהֵי אֲבוֹתֵינוּ, שֶׁהַמִּצְוָה שֶׁל הַפְרָשַׁת חַלָּה תֵּחָשֵׁב כְּאִלּוּ קִיַּמְתִּיהָ בְּכָל פְּרָטֶיהָ וְדִקְדּוּקֶיהָ, וְתֵחָשֵׁב הֲרָמַת הַחַלָּה שֶׁאֲנִי מְרִימָה, כְּמוֹ הַקָּרְבָּן שֶׁהִקְרַב עַל הַמִּזְבֵּחַ, שֶׁנִּתְקַבֵּל בְּרָצוֹן. וּכְמוֹ שֶׁלְּפָנִים הָיְתָה הַחַלָּה נְתוּנָה לַכֹּהֵן וְהָיְתָה זוֹ לְכַפָּרַת עֲוֹנוֹת, כָּךְ תִּהְיֶה לְכַפָּרָה לַעֲוֹנוֹתַי, וְאָז אֶהְיֶה כְּאִלּוּ נוֹלַדְתִּי מֵחָדָשׁ, נְקִיָּה מֵחֵטְא וְעָוֹן. וְאוֹכַל לְקַיֵּם מִצְוֹת שַׁבָּת קֹדֶשׁ וְהַיָּמִים הַטּוֹבִים עִם בַּעֲלִי (וִילָדֵינוּ), לִהְיוֹת נִזּוֹנִים מִקְּדֻשַּׁת הַיָּמִים הָאֵלֶּה. וּמֵהַשְׁפָּעָתָהּ שֶׁל מִצְוַת חַלָּה, יִהְיוּ יְלָדֵינוּ נִזּוֹנִים תָּמִיד מִיָּדָיו שֶׁל הַקָּדוֹשׁ בָּרוּךְ הוּא, בְּרֹב רַחֲמָיו וַחֲסָדָיו, וּבְרֹב אַהֲבָה, וְשֶׁתִּתְקַבֵּל מִצְוַת חַלָּה כְּאִלּוּ נָתַתִּי מַעֲשֵׂר. וּכְשֵׁם שֶׁהִנְנִי מְקַיֶּמֶת מִצְוַת חַלָּה בְּכָל לֵב, כָּךְ יִתְעוֹרְרוּ רַחֲמָיו שֶׁל הַקָּדוֹשׁ בָּרוּךְ הוּא לְשָׁמְרֵנִי מִצַּעַר וּמִמַּכְאוֹבִים כָּל הַיָּמִים, אָמֵן

Translation

May it be Your will, our God, the God of our Fathers, that the *mitzvah* of separating challah be considered as if I observed every one of its details. May my raising of the challah be considered as the sacrifice that was offered on the altar, which was willingly accepted. Just as giving the challah to the kohen in the past served to atone for sins, so may it atone for my sins, and I shall be like a person reborn, free of sin and transgression. May I be able to observe the holy Shabbat and Festivals [with my husband (and our children)], and be nourished from the holiness of these days. May the influence of the *mitzvah* of challah enable me [and my husband and (our children)] to always be nourished by the hands of the Holy One blessed be He, with His abundant mercy, loving-kindness, and great love; and the *mitzvah* of challah be accepted as though I have given a tithe. And now, as I am fulfilling the *mitzvah* of challah with all my heart, so may the compassion of the Holy One Blessed be He be aroused to keep me from sorrow and pain always, Amen.

The piece of dough must now be burned on an open fire until it is charred. If using a gas range, **double wrap the dough in aluminum foil** so that it doesn't touch the grate. Then discard the piece in the refuse bin. If you can't burn it, double wrap it in aluminum before discarding.

ROSH CHODESH PSALMS

It is customary in some circles to recite the following psalms as part of a Rosh Chodesh cohort of women.

Psalm 121

שִׁיר לַמַּעֲלוֹת אֶשָּׂא עֵינַי אֶל הֶהָרִים מֵאַיִן יָבֹא עֶזְרִי: עֶזְרִי מֵעִם ה׳ עֹשֵׂה שָׁמַיִם וָאָרֶץ: אַל יִתֵּן לַמּוֹט רַגְלֶךָ אַל יָנוּם שֹׁמְרֶךָ: הִנֵּה לֹא יָנוּם וְלֹא יִישָׁן שׁוֹמֵר יִשְׂרָאֵל: ה׳ שֹׁמְרֶךָ ה׳ צִלְּךָ עַל יַד יְמִינֶךָ: יוֹמָם הַשֶּׁמֶשׁ לֹא יַכֶּכָּה וְיָרֵחַ בַּלָּיְלָה: ה׳ יִשְׁמָרְךָ מִכָּל רָע יִשְׁמֹר אֶת נַפְשֶׁךָ: ה׳ יִשְׁמָר צֵאתְךָ וּבוֹאֶךָ מֵעַתָּה וְעַד עוֹלָם

A song for ascents. I shall raise my eyes to the mountains, from where will my help come? My help is from the Lord, the Maker of heaven and earth. He will not allow your foot to falter; Your Guardian will not slumber. Behold the Guardian of Israel will neither slumber nor sleep. The Lord is your Guardian; the Lord is your shadow; [He is] by your right hand. By day, the sun will not smite you, nor will the moon at night. The Lord will guard you from all evil; He will guard your soul. The Lord will guard your going out and your coming in from now and to eternity.

Psalm 150

הַלְלוּיָהּ! הַלְלוּ אֵל בְּקָדְשׁוֹ הַלְלוּהוּ בִּרְקִיעַ עֻזּוֹ: הַלְלוּהוּ בִגְבוּרֹתָיו הַלְלוּהוּ כְּרֹב גֻּדְלוֹ: הַלְלוּהוּ בְּתֵקַע שׁוֹפָר הַלְלוּהוּ בְּנֵבֶל וְכִנּוֹר: הַלְלוּהוּ בְתֹף וּמָחוֹל הַלְלוּהוּ בְּמִנִּים וְעֻגָב: הַלְלוּהוּ בְצִלְצְלֵי שָׁמַע הַלְלוּהוּ בְּצִלְצְלֵי תְרוּעָה: כֹּל הַנְּשָׁמָה תְּהַלֵּל יָהּ הַלְלוּיָהּ

Hallelujah! Praise God in His holy place, praise Him in the firmament of His might. Praise Him with His mighty deeds, praise Him as befits His superb greatness. Praise Him with a shofar blast, praise Him with psaltery and lyre. Praise Him with timbres and dance, praise Him with stringed instruments and flute. Praise Him with resounding cymbals, praise Him with resonant cymbals. Let every soul praise God. Hallelujah!

Psalm 67

לַמְנַצֵּחַ בִּנְגִינֹת מִזְמוֹר שִׁיר: אֱלֹהִים יְחָנֵּנוּ וִיבָרְכֵנוּ יָאֵר פָּנָיו אִתָּנוּ סֶלָה: לָדַעַת בָּאָרֶץ דַּרְכֶּךָ בְּכָל גּוֹיִם יְשׁוּעָתֶךָ: יוֹדוּךָ עַמִּים, אֱלֹהִים יוֹדוּךָ עַמִּים כֻּלָּם: יִשְׂמְחוּ וִירַנְּנוּ לְאֻמִּים כִּי תִשְׁפֹּט עַמִּים מִישׁוֹר וּלְאֻמִּים בָּאָרֶץ תַּנְחֵם סֶלָה: יוֹדוּךָ עַמִּים, אֱלֹהִים יוֹדוּךָ עַמִּים כֻּלָּם: אֶרֶץ נָתְנָה יְבוּלָהּ יְבָרְכֵנוּ אֱלֹהִים אֱלֹהֵינוּ: יְבָרְכֵנוּ אֱלֹהִים וְיִירְאוּ אוֹתוֹ כָּל אַפְסֵי אָרֶץ

For the conductor, with string-music; a psalm, a song. God will be gracious to us and bless us; He will cause His countenance to shine with us forever. That Your way should be known on earth, Your salvation among all nations. Peoples will thank You, O God; peoples will thank You, yea, all of them. Kingdoms will rejoice and sing praises, for You will judge peoples fairly, and the kingdoms — You will lead them on earth forever. Peoples will thank You, O God; peoples will thank You, yea, all of them. The earth gave forth its produce; God, our God, will bless us. God will bless us, and all the ends of the earth will fear Him.

WHAT YOU "KNEAD"
TO KNOW ABOUT CHALLAH

This chapter is an introduction to what you need to know about challah. Once you have formed your *Spiritual Kneading* group, the first meeting should cover this chapter before you move on to your Rosh Chodesh meetings. With this chapter giving more context, baking challah in celebration of Rosh Chodesh will become even more powerful and meaningful. That does not mean, of course, that Rosh Chodesh should be the only time we come together to bake challah. After all, challah is a primary component of every Shabbat and festival meal. This introductory chapter can also be used whenever women wish to come together to make challah, or even when they wish to make their own baking, at home, more meaningful.

NOTE: In this book, most of the challah recipes do not use eggs. In ancient times, challah was more like flat bread, similar to pita, and did not contain eggs. Many Sephardi Jews kept this custom, excluding eggs from their challah recipes. There is no right or wrong as to whether to include eggs in the challah; it is a matter of custom and preference. The addition of eggs to challah is a tradition from Ashkenazi Jews from Eastern Europe.

Suggested Ingredients:
In the invitation, ask participants to bring organic, fair trade ingredients for the challah.

Suggested Challah Recipe:
See *Basic Challah using Fresh Yeast*, page 150.

Suggested Challah:
Choose any Braided Challah Shape, page 158.

Visuals (optional):
A table set with a challah board, challah cover, bread knife, salt-shaker and Kiddush cup.

Introduction to Challah Theme during the Yeast Activation

The Significance of Challah

Baking challah is a fine illustration of the power of women to take raw ingredients and create something more, just as we are able to nurture a few tiny cells within our body and develop them into a living, breathing child. Baking challah is like raising a family or cultivating a relationship — it takes time and effort, but it is worth all the sacrifice.

We try and use the finest ingredients to make our challah, because every component contributes to the physical *and* spiritual quality of the final product, including how the ingredients are grown. Therefore, we are using organic and fair trade ingredients that have been grown with a holistic, ecological and balanced approach to farming. This connects us to the ancient roots of Judaism, which intertwined agriculture and worship, tying the most fundamental elements of life to a vision of divinity. The ingredients are imbued with this divinity, which passes into the challah we feed our family.

The first ingredient we will be using is fresh yeast, which is a live organism that needs tender loving care in order to grow — specifically, it needs to be fed sugar, traditionally seen as symbolic of love, and water, symbolic of Torah. Everyone needs positive input (love) to grow, but sometimes the sweetness we are given doesn't have an effect immediately — it needs time to incubate. The yeast needs ten minutes to "digest" love in order to grow. When the yeast is bubbling with joy, will we know that the sugar has been effective.

After the yeast has grown (activated), we will sift the flour. Adam, the first man, is referred to as the "challah of the world,"[1] because of the manner in which he was created — "God gathered dust [flour] and mixed it with water, creating a clay similar to dough." (Genesis 2:6) Then God breathed His Divine spirit into Adam, to give him a soul, elevating and uplifting him from what would have been a purely material existence. Similarly, when we unify the flour with the water, it can serve as a reminder that we need to be holy and sanctified in order to fulfill our role in God's world.

You will notice that the yeast has grown quite large, perhaps too much so for its own good. The sugar has inflated the yeast to the extent that it has become grandiose. To bring the yeast down to reality, we need to add a pinch of salt to cut the sweetness. In raising children, there needs to be a little pinch of discipline in order to help them get through life without losing hope or strength of character. However, this can only be done successfully when we *first* fortify them with the sweetness of love, empowering them to handle the necessary stringencies of the world.

 If using eggs to form the dough: eggs represent the continuous cycle of life, and therefore remind us to view ourselves as individuals within a greater framework — part of the Jewish nation. Eggs can also allude to the woman's special role in creation. She provides the egg, and space within her body for which a child can form.

Finally, when we are cultivating a loved one's growth, we need to be mindful of doing so gently. The oil we add to the dough has the ability to *soften*. Think of it softening us, making us sensitive to others' needs.

---

1 Bereishit Rabbah 14

We can find meaning not just in eating the bread we bake, but in the actual process of making it — and making it holy. As we work on the dough by kneading and stretching it, we can meditate on the role of Jewish women — to take the tangible, earthly world and raise it for a higher purpose. It takes skill and hard work to form challah correctly, but with weekly practice, challah after challah, we can perfect these offerings that will grace our Shabbat tables.

The rule for kneading is that the harder and longer you sweat at it, the better it will be. If you put all your strength into kneading, the consistency of the dough will change and become more refined, and ultimately, the challah will taste better. For any quality work, you need your whole body to be engaged. The power of your kneading does not stem from the strength in your arms, but rather from the strength of your love.

This introductory meditation is to connect your breath, which in Judaism is linked to your soul, with the physical act of kneading. We will be using the breath to focus and merge with the divine, as God breathed into Adam, giving him life. We will use a slow, methodical breathing technique, forming a rhythm with the kneading, as a springboard to reach deep into ourselves and try and connect with God.

- Start with gentle belly breathing from the nose. This allows you to have more control over your breath. Slowly inhale and exhale, pulling your breath all the way into your belly. Feel your belly expand.

- Be totally present as you slowly inhale and exhale. If your mind wanders, calmly bring it back. Continue to focus on your breath and just your breath. Feel the difference in temperature between how the air goes in and how it goes out.

- Continue belly breathing, counting to four in your head while you breathe in. Allow the inhaled breath to travel to the hidden corners of your soul, which is contained in your body. Breathe all the way into your limbs, traveling to your fingertips and further down to the tips of your toes. Hold it in for 2 seconds. That hold is a "kiss" from the Divine.

- On your out breath, slowly exhale from your mouth until the count of five.

- Continue to breathe this way, focused on each breath's purpose — to reach the Divine in you. Just focus on your breath and the counting in your head. Use the knead to focus your intention.

After the meditation is complete, smell a fragrant spice such as cloves to re-involve yourself with the physical world and help you feel grounded again.

Challah Customs and How They Came to Be

Now the time has come when we need to leave the dough alone. It needs to be kept warm and protected, away from outside influences, given its own space and time to grow and develop. If we keep uncovering it, poking at it or moving it, it will never rise. This is also the way we need to raise our children — we need to trust that we have put in the right ingredients, love and discipline, but at a certain point, they need to learn and grow on their own.

While we are waiting patiently for the challah to rise, we will take a fresh look at the traditions surrounding our Shabbat meals. Shabbat meals are *Se'udot Mitzvah* — obligatory festive meals. *Se'udot Mitzvah* are commanded as part of life cycle events such as circumcisions, bar/bat mitzvahs and weddings, and also on every Shabbat and festival. In order to qualify as a *Se'udat Mitzvah*, the meal must include bread — its presence *defines* the meal. Bread has always held an important role in Judaism: the generic Hebrew term for bread, *lechem*, is found seventy-five times in the Torah alone, with many more terms for specific types of bread also used frequently. In ancient Israel, bread was part of every meal, constituting at least fifty percent of the diet, and it therefore became an intrinsic part of any Jewish ritual that involves food. There are three *Se'udot Mitzvah* on Shabbat, one on Friday night, and two on Shabbat day. The first two meals, on Friday night and at lunchtime on Shabbat day, begin with *Kiddush*, the blessing over wine. Next comes the ritual washing of hands before bread, with the accompanying blessing. Two loaves grace the table, placed on a special board and under a special cover. When *hamotzi,* the blessing over bread is made, the challah is cut (or torn), and sprinkled with salt before being given out. Only after participants partake in wine and challah is the rest of the meal served. A meal with bread concludes with the *Birkat Hamazon,* Grace After Meals.[2]

Wine to Usher in the Shabbat Meal

At the beginning of the Shabbat meal, we recite the *Kiddush* prayer, publically proclaiming the sanctity of the day. By so doing, we are fulfilling a positive commandment to "remember" the Sabbath. In order to emphasize the significance of this verbal proclamation, the rabbis mandated that these words be recited over a cup of wine. Wine is the only liquid that has its own special blessing, because wine is meant to raise an ordinary or even extraordinary human event to a higher spiritual level.

Two Whole Challahs on the Table

Bread defines a *Se'udat Mitzvah*, but why is it necessary to have two whole loaves on the table? During Temple times, twelve loaves of bread (known as showbread) were present at all times on a special golden table that stood opposite the Menorah in the northern part of the Sanctuary. Two columns of six loaves

---

2   The third meal is of less importance than the first two; bread is still required, but it does not need to be in the form of whole loaves, and there is no *Kiddush*.

faced each other, remained on the table all week and were replaced with fresh ones on Shabbat. We grace our Shabbat tables with two whole loaves of challah to commemorate the two columns of showbread. Some people try and represent the twelve loaves of showbread by using braided challahs, with the total number of braids per meal or per Shabbat adding up to twelve.

When the Jews dwelled in the desert, they were fed with manna, "bread from heaven," which rained down upon them each day. On Shabbat, however, the manna did not descend. Rather, a double portion was granted on Friday: one portion for that day and another for Shabbat. We place two challahs on the Shabbat table to commemorate this double portion of the "heavenly bread" we ate in the desert.

Covering the Challah

Different kinds of food require different blessings, and there is a specific hierarchy that determines which blessing is to be said first. This means that when we start a meal, or are presented with a plate of food, there is a specific order in which we are supposed to take our first bites. Bread is the quintessential staple food, the proverbial "staff of life." If bread is part of a meal it is always eaten first — the blessing over bread takes precedence over every other blessing. The one exception to this rule is when we recite *Kiddush*, on Shabbat and festivals. *Kiddush* always comes first, because we are using the wine to consecrate the day, and not merely drinking the wine for its own sake. This creates a slight issue: How can we bless the wine — and make it a center of ceremonial importance, no less — when bread is higher in the hierarchy than wine? The simple solution is to "remove" the bread by concealing it from view, in other words, by placing a cover over the challah before *Kiddush* is said.

Challah is Encased in a Cover and a Cutting Board

There is another reason that we cover the challah, beyond concealing it from view. As we have already said, the two challahs on our Shabbat table are a tribute to the manna, the bread from heaven that God sent us in the desert. When the manna rained down from heaven, dew fell first *and* afterward, to protect it and preserve its freshness. We place the challahs on a special cutting board and underneath a special cover to envelop them, just as the dew enveloped the manna, reliving the manna miracle at our Shabbat table.

Custom of Holding the Challahs

With bread holding such great significance, it's not surprising that some heads of households place all ten of their fingers on the challah loaves while they recite the blessing. This practice stems from the Jerusalem Talmud, which states that man must do ten religious duties (agricultural obligations) before he can eat a piece of bread.[3] Placing all ten fingers on the challah loaves serves as a sign to God that he has fulfilled these duties. Although today most people do not toil the land for bread, we may still place our ten fingers on the loaves commemorating how Judaism emerged out of an agriculturally based community.

---

3 Jerusalem Talmud, Challah 1:6

Salting the Challah

Our Shabbat tables are considered to be our own personal altars. Just as the altar in the Temple was used for making offerings to God, so, today, we lay our tables with our finest linens and dishware, and eat our finest food, in honor of God's presence[4] at our Shabbat meal. As salt was offered with every sacrifice, we dip our bread in salt, reliving this experience over and over again. Moreover, salt is a great emblem of our relationship with our ancient heritage. Salt is the original preservative, and as such, represents the idea that we have continually been fed and nourished by our Judaism for thousands of years.

Customs on Cutting/Tearing Challah

In the Torah, God tells the Israelites that they are not to use any iron tools when building the altar in the Sanctuary: "And there shall you build an altar to the Lord your God, an altar of stones; you shall not lift up any iron tool upon them. You shall build the altar of the Lord your God of whole stones, and you shall offer burnt offerings upon it to the Lord your God" (Deuteronomy 27:5-6). The same held true when Solomon built the Temple. Since our homes are like the Temple, and our Shabbat tables like the altar, many Sephardi Jews have the custom of commemorating the prohibition against using cutting tools by tearing the challah, rather than cutting it with a knife. Some Sephardim throw the bread to each other, rather than passing it, to symbolize the manna that fell from the sky. Among Ashkenazi Jews, the custom is to cut the challah with a knife. There is no right or wrong way; it's just the custom of your family.

Kavanah for Hafrashat Challah

The first piece of dough that has been produced by all your hard work must be dedicated to God. The *mitzvah* of separating off a piece of the challah dough to be burned is done as a reminder that that portion would once have been given as a tithe to the *kohanim* who were serving God on our behalf, and therefore had no time to earn their own money or make their own bread. It also functions as a reminder that no matter how hard we work for it, our livelihood (our 'dough') is, in actuality, a gift from God.

The procedure and blessing for the *hafrashat challah* ceremony can be found on pages 14-18. Participants may wish to shape the challah afterwards, or take it home and shape it there.

---

4   In Ethics of our Fathers, (Pirkei Avot, 3:3) it is said that "three who eat at one table and speak words of Torah, it is as if they have eaten at God's table, as is stated, "And he said to me: This is the table that is before God" (Ezekiel 41:22).

THE SEGULAH CHALLAH BAKE

The Hebrew word *segulah* has many translations. It can mean remedy, merit, virtue and treasure. In this context, a *segulah* combines two of those meanings — it is participating in some kind of meritorious practice, a commandment or good deed, with the hope and intent that by doing so you will benefit from its positive spiritual effect. Some see *segulahs* as mere superstition, others as truly effective. There are many types of *segulah*, but often the idea of a particular *segulah* is that it will act as a remedy to alter a situation. For example, drinking the wine that is blessed during a *sheva brachot* celebration[1] is supposed to be a *segulah* for a single man or woman to find their partner, while participating in a circumcision ceremony by passing the baby to the *mohel* is a *segulah* to help a childless couple conceive.

There are several *segulah*s associated with separating challah. Doing this *mitzvah* is recognized as a *segulah* for an easy, safe birth; it is customary for Jewish women to separate challah at least once during their ninth month of pregnancy. There is also a popular custom of organizing forty or more women to participate in a shared challah bake with the intention of collectively dedicating the bake in the merit of a specific person who needs help, such as someone who is very ill, a woman struggling with infertility, or a person seeking their soul mate. When partaking in a *segulah* bake, it's important to pray for that person using their Hebrew name, together with the Hebrew name of their mother, if they are ill, or their father, otherwise choose a challah recipe and shape from the Appendices.

Introduction to Challah Theme during the Yeast Activation

The Power of Forty Women

The number forty in the Torah has special significance. It is connected with purity; for example, forty *se'ah*[2] of water are needed for a mikvah to be kosher. Moses ascended Mount Sinai for forty days to receive the Torah, during which time the Israelites had to emotionally cleanse themselves in order to be prepared to receive the holy commandments. The Great Flood of Noah's time lasted for forty days. These examples suggest that forty is the number required to make a significant change that supersedes nature. In choosing to do a *segulah* challah bake we must be mindful that the most important reason for the *segulah* is draw the Divine closer, and not just to try and alter someone's situation. It is through our special prayers and actions that we hope to bring God closer, because we are all united in the collective *tikkun* (spiritual repair) of our people, and this gladdens Him.

---

1   Sheva brachot celebrations take place for seven days after a wedding; they are parties for the new couple at which the seven blessings (sheva brachot) recited under the canopy are recited again at the end of the meal, over wine.

2   A se'ah is a unit of measurement equivalent to about 7.33 liters.

When pouring the water onto the yeast, ask God that Torah flow easily into your home, as water does from the heavens. As the yeast grows, be mindful of the person you are there for, and pray that their goods deeds, and yours, should always increase like the yeast.

While sifting the flour, imagine sifting your thoughts until your *kavanah* is focused solely on the person for whom you are doing the bake. If the gathering is in the merit of a sick person, ask God to expel (sift out) any sickness from the person.

When you add the sugar into the flour, ask God to sweeten His judgments for the person for whom you are gathering.

If using eggs to form the dough: eggs have many symbolic connotations. As a symbol of the circle of life, you can ask God to bless a sick person with the entire length of their years, and not have life cut short early. For someone who is struggling with infertility, you can ask God to bless that person with healthy eggs, so that at least one can take hold and become an embryo. Recognize that the egg is a reminder of our humble beginnings, that we all started the same way and therefore should always feel humility. We are never better than anyone else.

Oil is often used to soften; it softens skin, it makes things easier to glide over. Today we consider the oil in the challah as symbolic of asking God to soften His judgment, and yield to the needs of the person we are praying for.

Meditation during Kneading

We are all gathered here as part of the *segulah* challah bake to ask God to have mercy on the person we are praying for. We pray that any merit we may earn by doing this *mitzvah* should be bestowed upon them. We will meditate on the word *shalem*, meaning whole and complete. During the meditation, our *kavanah* will be focused on asking God to bring wholeness, *shleimut*, to the person in need.

- Begin with gentle belly breathing from the nose. This allows you to have more control over your breath. Slowly inhale and exhale, pulling your breath all the way into your belly. Feel your belly expand.
- Be totally present as you slowly inhale and exhale. If your mind wanders, calmly bring it back. Continue to focus on your breath and just your breath. Feel the difference in temperature between how the air goes in and how it goes out.
- Once you feel yourself enter a meditative state, direct your thoughts to the person's name and set it in your mind's eye. Hold it there for a moment.
- Draw down their name from your mind's eye to your heart. Focus on your *kavanah* for that person — that they should have completeness, *shleimut,* in their body and soul. Direct your love towards this person.

- Repeat their name, allowing the spiritual power of your request to filter through your mind and heart as it travels via your kneading hands to the dough.

After the meditation is complete, smell a fragrant spice such as cloves to re-involve yourself with the physical world, and help you feel grounded again.

Discussion during the Rising

A Treasured People — *Am Segulah*

"You are children of the Lord your God. You shall neither cut
yourselves nor make any baldness between your eyes for the dead.

For you are a holy people to the Lord your God, and the Lord has chosen you to
be a treasured people for Him, out of all the nations that are upon the earth."
(Deuteronomy 14:1-2)

In these verses, Moses is telling the Israelites that they are children of God. As such, they are not to mourn for the dead in too extreme a manner. Our God is Eternal; when our earthly parents die, we will not be orphans because God is our Father who watches over us, His very own "treasured people." The Hebrew word that is translated here as "treasured" is *segulah*. Here it means valuable personal property, guarded for safekeeping.

In addition to being a treasured people, the Jews were also called a chosen people. We were not chosen because of our ancestry, but in order to serve God through His commandments, to live in holiness and grace for the glory of God and for the welfare of the world. Our observance of the commandments will lead to *tikkun olam*, the spiritual repair of the world, and through that, God's goodness and love.

God's love is with us, and eternal, even when things seem at their worst. We are chosen and treasured that we may bring healing truth to the nations. Perhaps, therefore, a *segulah* practice might be understood as a person displaying a treasured connection with God by making some extra effort in their observance of the commandments. Baking challah in a cohort of forty women who are all focused on the same *kavanah* is a way of calling for God's help and mercy by practicing our faith in the way He demanded of us — united, as a community. As a group of women coming together with a prayer for someone else's wellbeing, we are expressing *chesed*, loving-kindness, one of God's own attributes.[3]

---

3 The Thirteen Attributes of Mercy are enumerated in Exodus 34:6-7, and are the attributes through which God governs the world.

Our Sages teach that it is the woman who brings blessings into her home through the vehicle of *hafrashat challah*. As it states in the Torah, "And the first of your dough you shall give to the *kohen*, in order that blessing will rest in your home" (Ezekiel 44:30). The procedure and blessing for the *hafrashat challah* ceremony can be found on pages 14-17. Since the Divine presence resting among us is strongest at this point, this is the most auspicious time to pray for the person in whose merit we have gathered here today. Immediately after separating the challah and saying the blessing, please recite the relevant prayer:

Refuah Sheleima — A Speedy Recovery

מִי שֶׁבֵּרַךְ אֲבוֹתֵינוּ אַבְרָהָם יִצְחָק וְיַעֲקֹב מֹשֶׁה וְאַהֲרֹן דָּוִד וּשְׁלֹמֹה הוּא יְבָרֵךְ אֶת הַחוֹלֶה [שם החולה
בן שם אמו] בַּעֲבוּר שֶׁאֲנִי אתפלל בַּעֲבוּרוֹ, בִּשְׂכַר זֶה הַקָּדוֹשׁ בָּרוּךְ הוּא יִמָּלֵא רַחֲמִים עָלָיו לְהַחֲלִימוֹ
וּלְרַפְּאֹתוֹ וּלְהַחֲזִיקוֹ וּלְהַחֲיוֹתוֹ, וְיִשְׁלַח לוֹ מְהֵרָה רְפוּאָה שְׁלֵמָה מִן הַשָּׁמַיִם לְרַמַ"ח אֵבָרָיו וּשְׁסַ"ה גִּידָיו
בְּתוֹךְ שְׁאָר חוֹלֵי יִשְׂרָאֵל, רְפוּאַת הַנֶּפֶשׁ וּרְפוּאַת הַגּוּף,הַשְׁתָּא בַּעֲגָלָא וּבִזְמַן קָרִיב. וְנֹאמַר אָמֵן:

Transliteration:

Mi Sheberakh Avoteinu: Avraham, Yitzhak, Yaakov, Moshe, Aharon, David v'Shlomo, Hu yivarekh virapei et haholeh/haholah _____ ben/bat (Mother's Name)_____ HaKadosh Barukh Hu yimalei rahamim alav/aleha, l'hahalimo/l'hahlimah, u-l'rap'oto/u-l'rap'otah, l'hahaziko/l'hazikah, u-l'hay-oto/u-l'hay-otah. V'yishlah lo/lah bim-hera r'fuah shlemah, r'fu-at hanefesh u-r'fu-at hagoof, b'tokh sh'ar holei Yisrael v'holei yoshvei tevel, hashta ba'agalah u-vizman kariv, v'no-mar, Amen

Translation:

May the One who blessed our ancestors — Patriarchs Abraham, Isaac, and Jacob, Moshe, Aharon, David and Shlomo — bless and heal the one who is ill: _____ son/daughter of (Mother's name)_____ . May the Holy Blessed One overflow with compassion upon him/her, to restore him/her, to heal him/her, to strengthen him/her, to enliven him/her. The One will send him/her, speedily, a complete healing — healing of the soul and healing of the body — along with all the ill, among the people of Israel and all humankind, soon, speedily, without delay, and let us all say: Amen!

Psalm 102

א תְּפִלָּה לְעָנִי כִי־יַעֲטֹף וְלִפְנֵי ה׳ יִשְׁפֹּךְ שִׂיחוֹ׃ ב ה׳ שִׁמְעָה תְפִלָּתִי וְשַׁוְעָתִי אֵלֶיךָ תָבוֹא׃ ג אַל־תַּסְתֵּר פָּנֶיךָ מִמֶּנִּי בְּיוֹם צַר לִי הַטֵּה־אֵלַי אָזְנֶךָ בְּיוֹם אֶקְרָא מַהֵר עֲנֵנִי׃ ד כִּי־כָלוּ בְעָשָׁן יָמָי וְעַצְמוֹתַי כְּמוֹקֵד נִחָרוּ׃ ה הוּכָּה כָעֵשֶׂב וַיִּבַשׁ לִבִּי כִּי־שָׁכַחְתִּי מֵאֲכֹל לַחְמִי׃ ו מִקּוֹל אַנְחָתִי דָּבְקָה עַצְמִי לִבְשָׂרִי׃ ז דָּמִיתִי לִקְאַת מִדְבָּר הָיִיתִי כְּכוֹס חֳרָבוֹת׃ ח שָׁקַדְתִּי וָאֶהְיֶה כְּצִפּוֹר בּוֹדֵד עַל־גָּג׃ ט כָּל־הַיּוֹם חֵרְפוּנִי אוֹיְבָי מְהוֹלָלַי בִּי נִשְׁבָּעוּ׃ י כִּי־אֵפֶר כַּלֶּחֶם אָכָלְתִּי וְשִׁקֻּוַי בִּבְכִי מָסָכְתִּי׃ יא מִפְּנֵי־זַעַמְךָ וְקִצְפֶּךָ כִּי נְשָׂאתַנִי וַתַּשְׁלִיכֵנִי׃ יב יָמַי כְּצֵל נָטוּי וַאֲנִי כָּעֵשֶׂב אִיבָשׁ׃ יג וְאַתָּה ה׳ לְעוֹלָם תֵּשֵׁב וְזִכְרְךָ לְדֹר וָדֹר׃ יד אַתָּה תָקוּם תְּרַחֵם צִיּוֹן כִּי־עֵת לְחֶנְנָהּ כִּי־בָא מוֹעֵד׃ טו כִּי־רָצוּ עֲבָדֶיךָ אֶת־אֲבָנֶיהָ וְאֶת־עֲפָרָהּ יְחֹנֵנוּ׃ טז וְיִירְאוּ גוֹיִם אֶת־שֵׁם ה׳ וְכָל־מַלְכֵי הָאָרֶץ אֶת־כְּבוֹדֶךָ׃ יז כִּי־בָנָה ה׳ צִיּוֹן נִרְאָה בִּכְבוֹדוֹ׃ יח פָּנָה אֶל־תְּפִלַּת הָעַרְעָר וְלֹא־בָזָה אֶת־תְּפִלָּתָם׃ יט תִּכָּתֶב זֹאת לְדוֹר אַחֲרוֹן וְעַם נִבְרָא יְהַלֶּל־יָהּ׃ כ כִּי־הִשְׁקִיף מִמְּרוֹם קָדְשׁוֹ ה׳ מִשָּׁמַיִם אֶל־אֶרֶץ הִבִּיט׃ כא לִשְׁמֹעַ אֶנְקַת אָסִיר לְפַתֵּחַ בְּנֵי תְמוּתָה׃ כב לְסַפֵּר בְּצִיּוֹן שֵׁם ה׳ וּתְהִלָּתוֹ בִּירוּשָׁלָיִם׃ כג בְּהִקָּבֵץ עַמִּים יַחְדָּו וּמַמְלָכוֹת לַעֲבֹד אֶת־ה׳׃ כד עִנָּה בַדֶּרֶךְ [כֹּחִי] (כֹּחוֹ) קִצַּר יָמָי׃ כה אֹמַר אֵלִי אַל־תַּעֲלֵנִי בַּחֲצִי יָמָי בְּדוֹר דּוֹרִים שְׁנוֹתֶיךָ׃ כו לְפָנִים הָאָרֶץ יָסַדְתָּ וּמַעֲשֵׂה יָדֶיךָ שָׁמָיִם׃ כז הֵמָּה יֹאבֵדוּ וְאַתָּה תַעֲמֹד וְכֻלָּם כַּבֶּגֶד יִבְלוּ כַּלְּבוּשׁ תַּחֲלִיפֵם וְיַחֲלֹפוּ׃ כח וְאַתָּה־הוּא וּשְׁנוֹתֶיךָ לֹא יִתָּמּוּ׃ כט בְּנֵי־עֲבָדֶיךָ יִשְׁכּוֹנוּ וְזַרְעָם לְפָנֶיךָ יִכּוֹן

Hear my prayer, O LORD, and let my cry come to You. Hide not Your face from me on the day when I am in trouble; incline Your ear to me. On the day when I call, answer me speedily, for my days are consumed like smoke, and my bones are burned as a hearth. My heart is smitten and withered like grass, so that I forget to eat my bread. By reason of the voice of my groaning, my bones cleave to my skin. I am like a pelican of the wilderness; I am like an owl of the desert. I watch, and am as a sparrow alone upon the housetop. My enemies reproach me all the day, and them that are mad against me are sworn against me. For I have eaten ashes like bread and mingled my drink with weeping, because of Your indignation and Your wrath; for You have lifted me up, and cast me down. My days are like a shadow that declines, and I am withered like grass. But You, O LORD, shall endure forever, and Your remembrance unto all generations. You shall arise and have mercy upon Zion; for the time to favor her, yea, the set time has come. For Your servants take pleasure in her stones, and favor the dust thereof. So the heathen shall fear the name of the LORD, and all the kings of the earth Your glory. When the LORD shall build up Zion, He shall appear in His glory. He will regard the prayer of the destitute, and not despise their prayer. This shall be written for the generation to come, and the people who shall be created shall praise the LORD. For He has looked down from the height of His sanctuary; from heaven did the LORD behold the earth, to hear the groaning of the prisoner, to free those that are appointed to death, to declare the name of the LORD in Zion, and His praise in Jerusalem, when people are gathered together, and the kingdoms, to serve the Lord. He weakened my strength on the way; He shortened my days. I said, "O my God, take me not away in the midst of my days; Your years are throughout all generations. Of old have You laid the foundation of the earth, and the heavens are the work of Your hands. They shall perish, but You shall endure; yea, all of them shall wax old like a garment; and as a vesture shall You change them, and they shall be changed. But You are the same, and Your years shall have no end. The children of Your servants shall continue, and their seed shall be established before You."

For Healthy Childbirth

Psalm 4

א לַמְנַצֵּחַ בִּנְגִינוֹת מִזְמוֹר לְדָוִד: ב בְּקָרְאִי עֲנֵנִי אֱלֹהֵי צִדְקִי בַּצָּר הִרְחַבְתָּ לִּי חָנֵּנִי וּשְׁמַע תְּפִלָּתִי: ג בְּנֵי־אִישׁ עַד־מֶה כְבוֹדִי לִכְלִמָּה תֶּאֱהָבוּן רִיק תְּבַקְשׁוּ כָזָב סֶלָה: ד וּדְעוּ כִּי־הִפְלָה ה׳ חָסִיד לוֹ ה׳ יִשְׁמַע בְּקָרְאִי אֵלָיו: ה רִגְזוּ וְאַל־תֶּחֱטָאוּ אִמְרוּ בִלְבַבְכֶם עַל־מִשְׁכַּבְכֶם וְדֹמּוּ סֶלָה: ו זִבְחוּ זִבְחֵי־צֶדֶק וּבִטְחוּ אֶל־ה׳: ז רַבִּים אֹמְרִים מִי־יַרְאֵנוּ טוֹב נְסָה־עָלֵינוּ אוֹר פָּנֶיךָ ה׳: ח נָתַתָּה שִׂמְחָה בְלִבִּי מֵעֵת דְּגָנָם וְתִירוֹשָׁם רָבּוּ: ט בְּשָׁלוֹם יַחְדָּו אֶשְׁכְּבָה וְאִישָׁן כִּי־אַתָּה ה׳ לְבָדָד לָבֶטַח תּוֹשִׁיבֵנִי:

For the chief musician for stringed instruments, a Psalm of David. Hear me when I call, O God of my righteousness! You have enlarged me when I was in distress; have mercy on me, and hear my prayer. Oh you sons of men, how long will you turn my glory into shame? How long will you love vanity, and seek after falsehood? (Selah.) But know that the Lord has set apart the pious man for himself; the Lord will hear when I call to him. Tremble, and do not sin; talk with your own heart on your bed, and be still. (Selah.) Offer the sacrifices of righteousness, and put your trust in the Lord. There are many who say, Who will show us good? Lord, lift up the light of your countenance upon us. You have put more gladness in my heart than they have whose grain and wine are increased. I will both lie down and sleep in peace; for you alone make me, Lord, dwell in safety.

Psalm 70

א לַמְנַצֵּחַ לְדָוִד לְהַזְכִּיר: ב אֱלֹהִים לְהַצִּילֵנִי ה' לְעֶזְרָתִי חוּשָׁה: ג יֵבשׁוּ וְיַחְפְּרוּ מְבַקְשֵׁי
נַפְשִׁי יִסֹּגוּ אָחוֹר וְיִכָּלְמוּ חֲפֵצֵי רָעָתִי: ד יָשׁוּבוּ עַל־עֵקֶב בָּשְׁתָּם הָאֹמְרִים הֶאָח הֶאָח: ה
יָשִׂישׂוּ וְיִשְׂמְחוּ בְּךָ כָּל־מְבַקְשֶׁיךָ וְיֹאמְרוּ תָמִיד יִגְדַּל אֱלֹהִים אֹהֲבֵי יְשׁוּעָתֶךָ: ו וַאֲנִי עָנִי
וְאֶבְיוֹן אֱלֹהִים חוּשָׁה לִּי עֶזְרִי וּמְפַלְטִי אַתָּה ה' אַל־תְּאַחַר:

To the chief Musician, a Psalm of David, to bring remembrance. Make haste, O God, to save me; make haste to help me, O Lord. Let those who seek after my soul be ashamed and confounded; let those who desire my harm be turned backward, and put to confusion. Let those who say Aha, aha, be turned back, because of their shame; Let all those who seek you rejoice and be glad in you; and let those who love your salvation say continually, Let God be magnified. But I am poor and needy; make haste to me, O God; you are my help and my savior; O Lord, delay not.

Participants may wish to shape the challah afterwards, or take it home and shape it there.

תשרי

Spiral Challah with Apple and Silan

Yields: 8 medium challahs

INGREDIENTS

4 tablespoons active dry yeast

2 tablespoons organic sugar

4 ½ cups (1.1 liters) warm water

5 pounds (2.25 kg) organic white flour

1 ½ tablespoons sea salt

1 12-ounce (350 g) container of Silan honey (date honey)

1 cup (230 ml) neutral-tasting oil, such as safflower oil

Apple Filling

4 crisp baking apples, such as Gala or Fuji, cored, peeled and diced into ¼-inch (½ centimeter) cubes

1 tablespoon packed brown sugar

1 teaspoon ground cinnamon

Topping

2 cage-free organic eggs, beaten

Cinnamon Sugar (combine equal parts)

Slivered Almonds

1 In a large bowl, combine the yeast with the 2 tablespoons of sugar and the warm water. Cover the bowl and allow the mixture to start activating. Yeast activation should take about 10 minutes; it will be bubbling and foamy.

2 Set 1 cup (125 g) of flour aside. Sift the remaining flour and salt into the bowl.

3 Pour the Silan honey and oil onto the flour. Combine all the ingredients, using a spatula. When it begins to form a dough, it is time to knead. At this point, you can remove the dough from the bowl and knead on the kitchen counter if it's easier for you, or directly in the bowl.

4 To knead the dough: grab the side of the dough furthest away from you and fold it toward yourself. Fold the dough in half and use your body weight to push the dough into itself. If you find that the dough is sticking too much to the surface and preventing you from kneading properly, dust some flour on the dough. Give the dough a quarter turn (90 degrees). Grab the other side and fold it in half. Again, with a lot of weight behind it, push the newly folded half into itself. Repeat this process for 10-15 minutes or until the dough is smooth, silky, elastic and the dough does not stick to the surface.

5 After the dough is thoroughly prepared, lay it on the countertop while you grease the bowl with a fine layer of oil. Next, turn the dough in the oil several times so that the dough is greased lightly on all sides.

6 Cover the bowl with a large plastic garbage bag or kitchen towel and allow it to rise for 1 hour.

7   In the meantime, combine the diced apples, sugar and cinnamon in a small bowl, tossing with a sprinkle of flour to coat. This will form apple syrup at the bottom of the bowl.

8   Make the blessing on *hafrashat challah* — see **Hafrashat Challah, page 17.**

9   Knead the dough again for a few minutes and then divide the dough into 8 equal parts. Use the remaining flour to flour surface area and hands to prevent sticking.

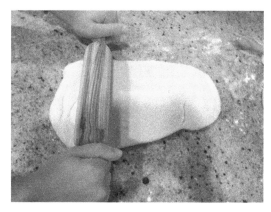

10 Using a rolling pin, roll each piece into a long narrow strand that is about 6 inches (15 cm) wide by 1 ½ feet (45 cm) long. Place a thin line of apples at the center of the flattened dough going all the way down until 2 inches (5 cm) from the ends.

11 Roll the strand until it becomes smooth, using gentle pressure with your hands on the center of the strand, pulling outward as you roll. Pinch the ends together. Re-flour the surface as needed to keep your dough from sticking.

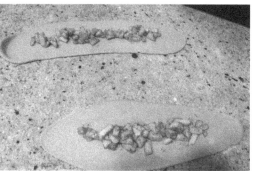

12 Starting from the tapered end, swirl the dough into a spiral.

13 Cover the loaves again and let them rise in a warm place for 1 hour, or until the dough has doubled in volume from its original size.

14 If you cannot bake the challah immediately, then this is the time to wrap the shaped dough in plastic wrap to prevent drying. You can store it in the coldest part of the refrigerator for up to 48 hours. On the day of baking, remove from refrigerator and let stand on kitchen counter until it reaches room temperature, about 1 hour.

15 Preheat oven to 350° F (180° C). Brush challah with beaten eggs and sprinkle with the cinnamon sugar and top with slivered almonds.

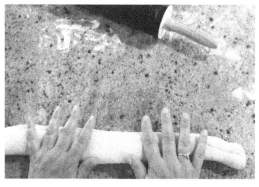

16 Bake in preheated oven for about 30-35 minutes, or until loaves turn golden brown and shiny. Bread should have a nice hollow sound when thumped on the bottom.

17 Remove from oven and cool on a rack. Wait at least 1 hour before serving. If you are freezing, wrap in waxed paper and foil and store in the freezer for up to 2 months. Serve warm or at room temperature.

Before Preparing the Dough, recite optional Rosh Chodesh Psalms, page 19.

Introduction to Challah Theme during the Yeast Activation

Teshuvah — Cleansing the Soul

After God created Adam and Eve, He placed them in the Garden of Eden, to "till it and to guard it" (Genesis 2:15). This "tilling" of the land of Eden was required of Adam and Eve for their own benefit. By undertaking a deed in the physical world, they became partners with God, deriving pleasure from knowing that they were contributing to the world's perfection. This Edenic tilling stands in marked contrast to the harsh, backbreaking work that Adam was required to do after he and Eve sinned and were exiled from Eden. Thereafter, God told him that the ground was cursed, that it would put forth thistles and thorns, and that he would only be able to eat bread by the sweat of his brow.[1] Making challah right after Rosh Hashanah, the anniversary of the creation, models the experience of Adam and Eve in Eden.

Rosh Hashanah overshadows the celebration of the New Moon, because Rosh Chodesh Tishrei *is* Rosh Hashana, a holy day when no baking can be done. Instead, it is fitting that we make challah on a regular day during the Ten Days of Repentance, which includes Rosh Hashanah, Yom Kippur, and the days between. This is a time when God is making a close accounting of our souls,[2] a beautiful gift from God that has been built into the blueprint of existence.[3] Making challah during this time is one way to start the New Year right. By doing so, we are showing our immense gratitude to God for giving us an opportunity to do *teshuvah* — the ability to reconnect to our truest, most wholesome selves. When baking challah is seen as simulating the experience of tilling, in Eden, the *mitzvah* becomes that much more transcendent.

There are many food traditions associated with Rosh Hashana and the month of Tishrei. On Rosh Hashana itself, we express the hope that we will be blessed with a sweet year by eating apple — a sweet fruit — dipped in honey. Why apples, rather than any other kind of fruit? One reason given is connected to the blessings that Isaac gave his son, Jacob. When Jacob approached Isaac, who was blind, Isaac noticed a sweet smell coming from him, and said, "See, the smell of my son is like the smell of a field which God has blessed" (Genesis 27:27). According to Rashi,[4] the smell that Jacob carried with him was that of the Garden of Eden — specifically, of apple trees. The Vilna Gaon[5] comments further that this encounter between Isaac and Jacob, when Isaac blessed Jacob, took place on Rosh Hashana.

This reference to the Garden of Eden, the birth point of humanity, suggests that through *teshuvah* we will be purified and will merit a return to Eden. Using apples in our challah alludes to the sweetness of this potential.

Another custom, that carries the entire length of the month of Tishrei, is to dip challah in honey, rather than the usual salt, at our Shabbat and festival meals. To honor this custom, I have added date honey (the honey that is referred to in the Torah) to this month's challah recipe.

We will shape the challahs in a spiral. The word *shana*, year, has the same root as *shinui*, which means change, or transformation. As the circle of the year turns, repeating the same seasons and holidays as the year before, we are

---

1 Genesis 3:17-19

2 Talmud, Rosh Hashanah 18a

3 Zohar II:161a "The Holy One, blessed be He, looked into the Torah and created the world"

4 Rashi's full name was Shlomo Yitzchaki (Rashi is the acronym of his name). He was a French rabbi who lived from 1040-1105, and is famed as the author of a comprehensive commentary on the Bible and the Talmud. He is considered the 'father' of all the commentaries that followed him.

5 The Vilna Gaon, Elijah ben Shlomo Zalman Kremer, 1720-1797, was the foremost Jewish leader and thinker of modern times. Through his commentaries he became one of the most familiar and influential names in rabbinic study since the Middle Ages.

presented with a choice: do we want this year to be a repetition of the last, or do we want to make a positive change? Hopefully we will make choices for positive change, and each year we will climb higher and higher, creating a spiritual spiral. The infinite nature of the spiral symbolizes our perpetual striving for perfection.

Once the challahs are shaped, we will top them with slivered almonds, *sha-ked* in Hebrew, which symbolize divine favor.[6] We pray that God finds favor in our actions during the past year and gives us another chance to fulfill His commandments in the coming year.

It would be most appropriate to use this challah for the *Seudah Mafseket* — the concluding meal before the Yom Kippur fast. Just as it is a *mitzvah* to fast on Yom Kippur, it is a *mitzvah* to eat on the eve of the fast, and traditionally, families will sit down to a large meal a couple of hours before the fast begins. This challah, prepared with the purest of intentions, could act as the opener to the meal you will share with your family, a meal which could be the opportunity for you to ask forgiveness from your family members for any ways in which you may have hurt them during the previous year. What better way to wipe the slate of interpersonal relationships clean as you prepare to enter the holiest day of the year.

Meditation during Kneading

The Talmud says that on Rosh Hashana, God inscribes everyone's names into one of three books; a book of the righteous, a book of the evil, and a book of those who are in-between. Those who are righteous are immediately inscribed for life and those who are evil are immediately inscribed for death, but judgment is suspended for those who are in-between; they have ten days in which to repent before Yom Kippur, when their judgment will be finalized.[7] The actions that can alter God's decree for those of us who are "in-between" (which we presume to be all of us) are *teshuvah* — a return to God, *tefilah* — prayer, and *tzedakah* — giving charity. The books — and the decrees — are sealed on Yom Kippur, which is why the traditional greeting for Yom Kippur is *"G'mar Chatimah Tovah"* which literally means "May you complete a good seal."

The Hebrew word for repentance, *teshuvah*, has two meanings. It means return, and yet it also means answer. This can allude to the idea that to return *is* to answer. Perhaps, that the return to God is an answer to him. This meditation is designed as a means to seek *teshuvah* through the action of kneading.

- Begin with gentle belly breathing from the nose. This allows you to have more control over your breath. Slowly inhale and exhale, pulling your breath all the way into your belly. Feel your belly expand.

- Be totally present as you slowly inhale and exhale. If your mind wanders, calmly bring it back.

- Continue to focus on your breath and just your breath. Feel the difference in temperature between how the air goes in and how it goes out.

- Once you feel yourself enter a meditative state, direct your thoughts to one misdeed you committed this past year. Don't let the thought overwhelm you with sadness. Rather, embody your regret through your kneading of the dough.

- You are trying to make things right now, through the *mitzvah* of challah. This challah brings you closer to God and to feeling at one with Him.

---

6 See Numbers 17: Aaron's rod miraculously sprouted almond blossoms, which identified Aaron as the one chosen by God to be high priest for the nation.

7 Rosh Hashana 32b

- Focus on how you can stop or avoid this harmful action as you go forward in the New Year. This is real *teshuvah*: a commitment to change. Pray for it. Stay focused on your commitment while you knead the dough.

After the meditation is complete, smell a fragrant spice such as cloves to re-involve yourself with the physical world, and help you feel grounded again.

Discussion during the Rising

Actions Speak Louder Than Words

The moon of Tishrei at the onset of Rosh Hashana is barely visible, yet that tiny sliver heralds the birth of a new year. The Ten Days of Repentance that begin the year are its labor pangs, and Yom Kippur marks the moment of the full rebirth of our identities, when we refashion and recreate ourselves anew. On Yom Kippur, we abstain from food and drink and remove ourselves from luxury and physical pleasures so that the spiritual yearning for God has the potential to increase.[8] We are given a full day to rest, not just from our jobs, but also from our physical appetites. Ideally, fasting on Yom Kippur demonstrates to us that we have the ability to live in a state above our physical desires. This can make it easier for us to aspire to live at a higher level of spirituality during the rest of the year. Removing these physical distractions is an attempt to commune with God, asking Him to help us implement the changes we need to make a better life possible.

The term Yom Kippur is actually written in the plural in the Torah,[9] as *Yom Ha-Kippurim.* The plural form may have been used to suggest that there are many roads to atonement, as every individual is different and on a unique spiritual level. It may direct us to the fact that we each have multiple atonements to make, depending on our actions. Or perhaps it is because the purification process of *teshuvah* has four steps. [10]

We all go through periods when we lack awareness and mindfulness. Consequently, our actions move out of alignment with the will of God. We sin, and become estranged from all that we hold most dear at our core. Rousing ourselves from this spiritual apathy and doing *teshuvah* reactivates the essential connection point between our Creator and us.

The first step to *teshuvah* is confession, *vidduy.* This entails examining our lives honestly, admitting our mistakes and the possibility that we have wasted opportunities for growth. One method of doing this is to analyze our lives in separate eras — childhood, teen years, young adulthood, middle age, etc, and in separate categories — studies, romantic relationships, career, parenting, friendships and so on. When we look at the negative things we have done, we must look for patterns.

Once we have a sense of what the patterns look like, we can begin to understand and articulate not only the actions that we have come to regret, but also, the underlying causes of those actions. The purpose of this soul searching is not to tell God something that He didn't know. It is to help us regain our identities by seeing ourselves as we are. Then we can ask God to help us heal the damage we have done to ourselves. When we verbally confess, we are starting to uproot the negative impulses that drive us. It is a type of mental and spiritual *mikvah* — a cleansing of the soul — which is a necessary precursor for the next level of *teshuvah.*

---

8 This is extrapolated from the verse in the Kuzari written by Yehuda HaLevi, who was a Spanish poet, physician and philosopher (1075 — 1141): "The fast of this day is such as brings one near to the angels, because it is spent in humility and contrition, standing, kneeling, praising and singing. All his physical faculties are denied their natural requirements, being entirely abandoned to religious service, as if the animal element had disappeared. The fast of a pious man is such that eye, ear, and tongue share in it, that he regards nothing except that which brings him near to God. This also refers to his innermost faculties, such as mind and imagination. To this he adds pious works." (Kuzari 3:5)

9 Vayikra (Leviticus) 23:27

10 Maimonides, Hilchot Teshuvah, chapters 1 and 2

The second step is regret, *charata*, which entails a disassociation with the negative patterns to the point where they become demystified and an unacceptable way of being. Regret creates redefinition, leading to a release from the prison of self-limiting behavior. Feeling regret marks the end of the old order and neutralizes the inner feeling that compelled us to sin in the first place.

When we experience true regret, we move on automatically to the third level of *teshuvah* — abandonment, *aziva*. At this stage we stop dwelling on the transgression, in thought and in action. Abandoning a harmful behavior or sin means staying away from *all* the paths that lead to that negativity. This includes crafting our environments to prevent temptation. We can surround ourselves with wise people. Sublimate negative behaviors into creative ones. Celebrating Rosh Chodesh is on the continuum. Baking challah is a start.

The last step in the process of *teshuvah* is the resolution, *kabalah*[11] — accepting changes within ourselves that are so real that the old patterns over time will slowly fade away. We resolve upon a course of action — a plan to avert bad habits in the future. The goal is not to completely eradicate our bad habits all at once, but rather to have a plan in place that moves us to a gradual self-transcending reconfiguration of the soul.

Turn to God directly, openly, passionately and in your own language. Ask Him to free you from the prison you have erected around yourself. Tell Him where you have been, what you have done, and how you now know that you have done great harm to yourself and to others. Tell Him about the times you have tried to change and failed, and how you acknowledge that He loves you and has given you life. Ask him to help you see the answers clearly so that you can avert big mistakes in you life.

---

11 In the context here, it should not to be confused with the esoteric texts of Judaism, but rather on its literal translation, which means, to receive.

Reflective Questions

1. What does the word *teshuvah* imply? If it means to return, what are you returning from?

2. How can you explain the order of the *teshuvah* process? Do you think this order matters?

3. Is it human nature to avoid looking at your faults? A true *cheshbon hanefesh* (accounting of the soul, deep self-examination) can force you to contend with things that you might prefer to avoid. How do you convince yourself this is a worthwhile process? Is it possible to avoid the pain?

4. Is it possible to completely avoid evil desires? If yes, then how? And if not, what purpose do you think they serve in this world; why would God create them?

5. When do you most feel that your life is meaningful?

6. If you knew you could not fail, what would you undertake?

Kavanah for Hafrashat Challah

Tilling the land as Adam and Eve did within the Garden of Eden reflected the natural partnership with God that was required for their own benefit, one that contributed to the world's perfection. The *mitzvah* of separating challah offers women a unique opportunity to reflect on that perfect relationship with God through using the physical world, and thereby consecrating it to Him, that we may find our rightful place in Gan Eden once again.

The procedure and blessing for the hafrashat challah ceremony can be found on pages 14-17. Participants may wish to shape the challah afterwards, or take it home and shape it there.

CHESHVAN

Rainbow-shaped Challah

Yields: 6 large challahs

INGREDIENTS

Ingredients

4 tablespoons active dry yeast

4 ½ cups (1.1 liters) warm water

¾ cup (150 g) organic sugar plus 2 tablespoons
organic sugar

5 pounds (2.25 kg) organic white flour

1 cup (230 ml) neutral-tasting oil, such as
safflower oil

1 ½ tablespoons sea salt

Topping

maple syrup, for glaze
Rainbow sprinkles or colored sanding sugar

1 In a large bowl, combine the yeast with the 2 tablespoons of sugar and the warm water. Cover the bowl and allow the mixture to start activating. Yeast activation should take about 10 minutes; it will be bubbling and foamy.

2 Set 1 cup (125 g) of flour aside. Sift the remaining flour, sugar, and salt into the bowl.

3 Pour the yeast mixture and oil onto the flour. Combine all the ingredients, using a spatula. When it begins to form a dough, it is time to knead. At this point, you can remove the dough from the bowl and knead on the kitchen counter if it's easier for you, or directly in the bowl.

4 To knead the dough: grab the side of the dough furthest away from you and fold it toward yourself. Fold the dough in half and use your body weight to push the dough into itself. If you find that the dough is sticking too much to the surface and preventing you from kneading properly, dust the dough with flour. Give the dough a quarter turn (90 degrees). Grab the other side and fold it in half. Again, with a lot of weight behind it, push the newly folded half into itself. Repeat this process for 10-15 minutes, or until the dough is smooth, silky, elastic and the dough does not stick to the surface.

5 After the dough is thoroughly prepared, lay it on the countertop while you grease the bowl with a fine layer of oil. Next, turn the dough in the oil several times so that the dough is greased lightly on all sides.

6 Cover the bowl with a large plastic garbage bag or kitchen towel and allow it to rise for 1 hour.

7 Make the blessing on *hafrashat challah* — see **Hafrashat Challah, page 17.**

8 Knead the dough again for a few more minutes and then divide the dough into 16 equal parts. Use the remaining flour to flour the surface area and hands to prevent sticking.

9 Using a rolling pin, roll each piece into a long narrow strand.

10 You will need to cut these strands, as needed, to assemble the shape of a seven ray rainbow.

11 Start from the smallest ray, and modify each strand larger than the former to form the rainbow.

12 Cover the loaves again and let them rise in a warm place for 1 hour or until the dough has doubled in volume from its original size.

13 If you cannot bake the challahs immediately, then this is the time to wrap the shaped dough in plastic wrap to prevent drying. You can store it in the coldest part of the refrigerator for up to 48 hours. On the day of baking, remove the dough from refrigerator and let stand on kitchen counter until it comes to room temperature, about one hour.

14 Preheat the oven to 350° F (180° C). Brush your challahs with maple syrup and top with rainbow sprinkles or colored sanding sugar.

15 Bake in your preheated oven for about 35-40 minutes, or until loaves turn golden brown. Bread should have a nice hollow sound when thumped on the bottom.

16 Remove from the oven and cool on a rack. Wait at least one hour before serving. If you are freezing the challah, wrap in waxed paper and foil. It can be stored in the freezer for up to 2 months.

Before Preparing the Dough, recite optional Rosh Chodesh Psalms, page 19.

Introduction to Challah Theme during the Yeast Activation

Contemplation

The emphasis in this months' challah ingredient is water, which reflects the themes of rain and the Great Flood. The first prayer of the year on the subject of rain is actually said in the synagogue on *Shemini Atzeret*, the 22nd of Tishrei, and a shortened form is added to the second paragraph of the *Amidah* (central Jewish prayer said three times a day) from that date on, but that prayer is an *acknowledgment* of rain as God's blessing and province, and not an active *request* for rain.[1] In Israel, the country for which the Jewish calendar was created, actual praying *for* rain begins on the seventh of Cheshvan.[2] The words "*v'ten tal u'matar livrachah,*" which mean "and bestow dew and rain for blessing," are added to the ninth paragraph of the Amidah. Beyond the physical connection to the beginning of the rainy season, it is no coincidence that this prayer for rain is inserted right after Tishrei, when we planted the seeds of our promises to God. We hope that the blessing of rain should bring growth not only to the physical world, but to the spiritual world.

According to Rabbi David Kimchi (known as the RaDaK),[3] rainfall increases this month because the Great Flood of Noah's generation began in Cheshvan.[4] According to Rashi, the generation of the Flood was guilty of three things. They committed idolatry, they were guilty of all manner of sexual impropriety, including incest and violent theft was rampant. The Tosefta, contemporaneous with the Mishna, writes that the generation of the Flood acted arrogantly before God, scoffing that all they needed Him for was for a few drops of rain, deluding themselves into thinking that the rivers and wells they had were more than enough for their needs.[5] They failed to recognize that only God bestows "dew and rain for blessing." This conceit ultimately became the very tool of their destruction in the Flood. Rashi explains that even at the end, God gave them a last chance to atone: "He brought them [the rains] down with mercy, so that if they would repent, they [the rains] would be rains of blessing. When they did not repent, they became a flood."[6] We understand from this interpretation that there is a direct connection between how people act, and the rains that come into the world.

The Hebrew word for rain — *geshem* — is the root of the word *gashmiut*, which means physicality. The physical world is meant to sustain us so that we can develop an even greater connection with our Creator. Rain is a physical blessing that God grants us in order to bring us to our spiritual potential.

As we pour water into the flour to create our dough, we should be mindful of its source. While the flour can represent our earthly labor, when we combine the water and flour — the upper realm with the lower realm, we are raising our *gashmiut*, the physical manifestation of our life force, closer to its very source — God.

---

1 The Mishna says "On the festival of Sukkot, the rainfall of the world is judged," (Rosh Hashanah 1.2). We start mentioning the rain on Shemini Atzeret, and not the beginning of the Sukkot, as if it fell during Sukkot we would not be able to sit in the Sukkah.

2 The seventh of Cheshvan is fifteen days after Shemini Atzeret. Historically speaking, fifteen days would have been enough time for all the pilgrims who went to Jerusalem for Sukkot to get home again before the rains started, which is why that date was chosen. In the rest of the world, the prayer for rain is only added in December, as the need for rain is not as urgent elsewhere.

3 RaDaK (1160–1235), Rabbi David Kimchi (Rashi's grandson) was a medieval rabbi, biblical commentator, philosopher, and grammarian.

4 "In the eleventh year, during the month of Bul — which is the eighth month — the Holy Temple was completed according to all of its details and halachot. It took seven years [to finish]." (Kings I 6:38) Radak explains that the month referred to here is Cheshvan, the eighth month counting from Nissan. "It is called Bul," writes Radak, "because during this month, the flood activity begins."

5 Tosefta Sotah 3:6-8

6 Rashi on Genesis 7:12 "And the rain was upon the earth for forty days and forty nights."

When the Great Flood ended, God swore never again to bring a flood upon the earth to destroy all mankind, and revealed the sign of this covenant as the rainbow (Genesis 9:8–11). The rainbow, which in Hebrew is *keshet,* sounds similar to the word *kesher,* meaning connection. The word *kesher* sounds similar to *gesher,* meaning bridge in Hebrew. I like to think that these three words are intermingling to express the broader message of the rainbow — a colorful bridge that connects the earth to God and His promise. To commemorate this covenant, we are shaping the challahs as a seven-ray rainbow and using rainbow sprinkles or colored sanding sugar as a topping for our challahs, representing the entire spectrum of the rainbow's colors.

There are no festivals in the month of Cheshvan; it can be a month of contemplation set to the tone of gentle raindrops. As the days grow shorter, the moon shines longer, it's a time to go inwards into that dream state of the year, and think about the commitments we made during the month of Tishrei and how we will "water" them to fruition.

Meditation during the Kneading

Imagine the rain gently tapping down to earth from the sky to set a contemplative tone on how to proceed from the highs of Tishrei. We will be doing a mantra meditation; the repeated recitation of a verse. Whether whispered out loud or focused on silently, the mantra meditation initiates a relaxed state of consciousness so that the mind can enter into a conversation with God. You might want to ask Him how to actualize the changes you promised in Tishrei. When the mind is quiet and the heart attentive, God gives spiritual light. The mantra is *v'ten tal u'matar livrachah.*

- Start with gentle belly breathing from the nose. This allows you to have more control over your breath. Slowly inhale and exhale, pulling your breath all the way into your belly. Feel your belly expand.

- Be totally present as you slowly inhale and exhale. If your mind wanders, calmly bring it back.

- Continue to focus on your breath and just your breath. Feel the difference in temperature between how the air goes in and how it goes out.

- Once you feel yourself enter a meditative state, direct your thoughts to the verse, *v'ten tal u'matar livrachah* (bestow dew and rain for blessing).

- Repeat the verse, allowing the spiritual power of your request to filter through your mind and heart as it travels via your kneading hands — the *gashmiut* — to the dough.

- As your physicality is released into the dough and your thoughts are quieted by the power of the meditation, in that state of stillness focus on asking God how to integrate and take the insights you've received during the holidays of Tishrei into your daily routine. You might want to ask how can you turn your thoughts into physical deeds. Ask God to "water" the seeds of your thoughts so that they can grow.

After the meditation is complete, smell a fragrant spice such as cloves to re-involve yourself with the physical world and make you feel grounded again.

Discussion during The Rising

Our Foremother Rachels' Yahrtzeit

It is traditional to read about our matriarch Rachel's death on her *yahrtzeit,* the anniversary of her death, which is on the eleventh of Cheshvan.

Genesis 35:14-26

Ya'akov set up a standing-stone in the place where he had spoken with Him, a stone pillar. Then he poured out a drink offering on it and poured oil on it. Ya'akov called the place where God spoke with him Beit-El. Then they traveled on from Beit-El, and while there was still some distance to go before arriving in Efrat, Rachel went into labor, and she had great difficulty with it. While she was undergoing this hard labor, the midwife said to her, "Don't worry, this is also a son for you." As her soul was departing, for she died, she named her son Ben-Oni [son of my grief], but his father called him Binyamin [son of the right hand, son of the south]. So Rachel died and was buried on the way to Efrat (that is, Beit-Lechem). Ya'akov set up a standing-stone on her grave; it is the standing-stone of Rachel's grave to this day. Israel continued his travels and pitched his tent on the other side of the tower of Eder. It was while Israel was living in that land that Reuven went and slept with Bilhah, his father's concubine, and Israel heard about it. Ya'akov had twelve sons. The sons of Leah were Reuven, Ya'akov's firstborn, Shimon, Levi, Yehudah, Yissachar and Zevulun. The sons of Rachel were Yosef and Binyamin. The sons of Bilhah, Rachel's maidservant: Dan and Naphtali. The sons of Zilpah, Leah's maidservant: Gad and Asher. These are Jacob's sons who were born to him in Padan aram.

We do not know the *yahrtzeit* dates of the remaining forefathers and foremothers, however the date of Rachel's passing is known to us.[1] Since ancient times she has been seen as the epitome of a Jewish mother. This raises the question: What was it about Rachel's life and character that

made her, above the other foremothers, the embodiment of the Jewish ideals of motherhood? Rachel did not have an easy time achieving motherhood, and for much of her married life she had to watch her sister Leah have many children with Jacob (the love of Rachel's life), while she remained barren. She herself finally gave birth to Joseph. Only a few short years afterward she died while giving birth to Benjamin, en route to Bethlehem.

Jeremiah, the prophet who foresaw and bitterly lamented the destruction of the Temple and the exile of the Jews to Babylonia, described Rachel as a loving mother, weeping for her children as they stumble, chained, towards exile: "A voice is heard in Ramah, lamentation and bitter weeping. It is Rachel weeping for her children, she refuses to be comforted for her children, for they are gone" (Jeremiah 31:14). Yet Rachel's anguish is answered; God replies to her, "Refrain your voice from weeping and your eyes from tears: for your work shall be rewarded… there is hope for your future, and your children shall return again to their borders" (31:15-16).[2]

There is a *midrash* which states that Rachel was buried separately from the rest of the forefathers and foremothers precisely so that she could be well-placed to cry for the exiles on their dispirited march, and they could pray at her tomb for comfort. This seems to attribute to her a special connection to "her children." It's quite plausible that "Rachel crying for her children" doesn't only refer to Joseph and Benjamin, her biological children, but rather all of the twelve tribes, as God replies, "your *children* shall return to their borders."

An elaboration on the details surrounding Jacob and Rachel's impending nuptials may help us understand how Rachel earned the right to be seen as the quintessential mother. When Jacob met Rachel, he fell in love with her at first sight, and agreed to work for her father, Lavan, for

---

1 The source for this is a medieval midrash, the Yalkut Shimoni, which lists the birth dates of all the twelve sons of Jacob. It gives Benjamin's birthday as the eleventh of Cheshvan, and since Rachel died giving birth to him, this is presumed to be her Yahrzeit.

---

2 This is recited during the haftarah on the second day of Rosh Hashanah.

seven years, so that he could marry her. When seven years had passed, a wedding feast was arranged, but when night fell, Lavan led his elder daughter, Leah, to Jacob's bed, instead of Rachel. The *midrash* explains that Rachel spared her sister Leah from discovery and humiliation by telling her of the secret signs she had shared with Jacob to prevent just such a situation from occurring.[3] Rachel's sacrifice allowed her sister Leah to marry first, and to become the mother of Jacob's first children. It is possible to say, therefore, that Rachel was a mother even before she gave birth. Even barren women can be fruitful through their good deeds. The "children" God is referring to as He consoles Rachel are all of the twelve tribes, since even Leah's children were born through the merit of her compassion and sacrifice — two attributes of a good Jewish mother.

At the moment when Rachel passes on, and the darkness closes in, Benjamin is born. The only one of Jacob's children to be born in the Land of Israel, his birth heralds a new era, one that reflects the Jewish people's true destiny, of living in the Promised Land.

For thousands of years, Rachel's Tomb, on the outskirts of Bethlehem, has been a place of pilgrimage, for Jewish women in particular. It is traditional to go there to pray on her *yahrtzeit*, and on Rosh Chodesh. Rachel's unbounded and sorrowful love for her children draws people to her tomb to this day.

Interestingly, Rachel has a linguistic connection with baking: Bet Lechem (Bethlehem), where she died and was buried, means 'house of bread.' Perhaps in those days, fields of wheat surrounded Bethlehem.[4] Rachel's tears may have watered the wheat fields that would provide sustenance to her future generations. As it is traditional for women to visit Rachel's Tomb every Rosh Chodesh, how much more appropriate is it for us to bring her into our thoughts on the Rosh Chodesh of the month she died, while baking our challah.

Reflective Questions

1. What significance does water hold for you? Is it just about cleanliness? What do you know of its significance in the Torah?

2. Can you think of other events that took place in Biblical times where water was a theme? Any significant plot that stands out in your mind?

3. What does water represent to you? Aside from the practicality of it.

4. Why do you think God planned for us to know Rachel's burial site?

5. Can you learn anything from Rachel's anguish?

6. What is your focus for this month? How are you going to actualize the promises you made in Tishrei?

Kavanah for Hafrashat Challah

Rain has the ability to take a seed — something inert — and stimulate it to produce a living thing. Ask God to send rain in the merit of our foremother, Rachel, to nurture the physical world we depend upon, and to nurture our souls with the waters of Torah.

The procedure and blessing for the hafrashat challah ceremony can be found on pages 14-17. Participants may wish to shape the challah afterwards, or take it home and shape it there.

---

3   Tanhuma, Midrash, [ed. Buber], Vayetze 6

4   In the Book of Ruth, Ruth met Boaz in Bethlehem while picking wheat sheaths from his field.

KISLEV

כסלו

NOTE: There are two options for this month's challah: the Cheese Loaf Challah, which is dairy, and the Flame Challah, which is non-dairy. There is a halachic (Jewish law) ruling that it's generally not permissible to bake dairy challah, lest one err and eat it with a meat meal. Therefore, the *Code of Jewish Law* (Shulchan Aruch, YD 97:1) states that when baking dairy challah, one must make it look significantly different than regular challah, as in a different shape, bake a small amount that will likely be consumed at the meal, thereby minimizing the possibility of the leftover inadvertently getting eaten with meat, and take precautions to make sure its dairy nature is clearly marked.

Cheese Loaf

Yields: 6 long loaves

INGREDIENTS

¾ cup (150 g) organic sugar plus 2 tablespoons organic sugar

4 ½ cups (1.1 liters) warm water

4 tablespoons active dry yeast

5 pounds (2.25 kg) organic white flour

1 ½ tablespoons sea salt

1 cup (230 ml) extra virgin olive oil

Filling

20 ounces (600 g) feta cheese, crumbled

Za'atar (Middle Eastern blend of herbs, sesame and salt), optional

Topping

Olive oil, for glaze

Sesame seeds

1. In a large bowl, combine the yeast with the 2 tablespoons of sugar and the warm water. Cover the bowl and allow the mixture to start activating. Yeast activation should take about 10 minutes; it will be bubbling and foamy.

2. Set 1 cup (125 g) of flour aside. Sift the remaining flour, sugar, and salt into the bowl.

3. Pour the yeast mixture and oil onto the flour. Combine all the ingredients, using a spatula. When it begins to form a dough, it is time to knead. At this point, you can remove the dough from the bowl and knead on the kitchen counter if it's easier for you, or directly in the bowl.

4. To knead the dough: grab the side of the dough furthest away from you and fold it toward yourself. Fold the dough in half and use your body weight to push the dough into itself. If you find that the dough is sticking too much to the surface and preventing you from kneading properly, dust the dough with flour. Give the dough a quarter turn (90 degrees). Grab the other side and fold it in half. Again, with a lot of weight behind it, push the newly folded half into itself. Repeat this process for 10-15 minutes, or until the dough is smooth, silky, elastic and the dough does not stick to the surface.

5. After the dough is thoroughly prepared, lay it on the countertop while you grease the bowl with a fine layer of oil. Next, turn the dough in the oil several times so that the dough is greased lightly on all sides.

6. Cover the bowl with a large plastic garbage bag or kitchen towel and allow it to rise for 1 hour.

7. Make the blessing on *hafrashat challah* — see **Hafrashat Challah, page 17**

8. Knead the dough again for a few more minutes and then divide the dough into 8 equal parts. Use the remaining flour for the surface area and hands to prevent sticking.

9   With a rolling pin, roll out the dough into long ovals measuring roughly 16 inches (40 cm) long by 8 inches (20 cm) wide.

10 Use a sharp knife to cut strips 1 ½ inches (4 cm) wide, all the way down the side of the dough, on the diagonal, like a feather.

11 Place some feta cheese and za'atar (if using) in a strip down the center of each oval, leaving a little space at the top and bottom of the dough to fold it over the filling.

12 Overlap one strip from each side over the other side, in an X pattern creating the illusion of a braid. The filling will show through.

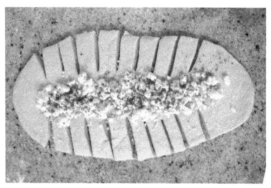

13   Cover the loaves again and let them rise in a warm place for 1 hour or until the dough doubles in volume.

14 If you cannot bake the challah immediately then this is the time to wrap the shaped dough in plastic wrap to prevent drying. You can store it in the coldest part of the refrigerator for up to 48 hours. On the day of baking, remove from refrigerator and let stand on kitchen counter until it reaches room temperature, about 1 hour.

15 Preheat oven to 350° F (180° C). Brush challah with olive oil and sprinkle with sesame seeds.

16 Bake in preheated oven for about 30-35 minutes, or until loaves turn golden brown and shiny. Bread should have a nice hollow sound when thumped on the bottom.

17 Remove from oven and cool on a rack. Wait at least 1 hour before serving. If you are freezing, wrap in waxed paper and foil and store in the freezer for up to 2 months. Serve warm or at room temperature. Before serving this challah, you might want to give it another wash with the olive oil if the glaze has dried out.

Before Preparing the Dough, recite optional Rosh Chodesh Psalms, page 19.

Flame-shaped Challah with Corn Grits

Yields: 10 small to medium challahs

INGREDIENTS

4 tablespoons active dry yeast

4 ½ cups (1.1 liters) warm water

¾ cup (150 g) organic sugar plus 2 tablespoons organic sugar

5 pounds (2.25 kg) organic white flour

1 ½ tablespoons sea salt

1 cup (250 ml) extra virgin olive oil

Topping

2 cage-free organic eggs, beaten

Corn grits, for topping

1 In a large bowl, combine the yeast with the 2 tablespoons of sugar and the warm water. Cover the bowl and allow the mixture to start activating. Yeast activation should take about 10 minutes; it will be bubbling and foamy.

2 Set 1 cup (125 g) of flour aside. Sift the remaining flour, sugar, and salt into the bowl.

3 Pour the yeast mixture and oil onto the flour. Combine all the ingredients, using a spatula. When it begins to form a dough, it is time to knead. At this point, you can remove the dough from the bowl and knead on the kitchen counter if it's easier for you, or directly in the bowl.

4 To knead the dough: grab the side of the dough furthest away from you and fold it toward yourself. Fold the dough in half and use your body weight to push the dough into itself. If you find that the dough is sticking too much to the surface and preventing you from kneading properly, dust the dough with flour. Give the dough a quarter turn (90 degrees). Grab

the other side and fold it in half. Again, with a lot of weight behind it, push the newly folded half into itself. Repeat this process for 10-15 minutes, or until the dough is smooth, silky, elastic and the dough does not stick to the surface.

5   After the dough is thoroughly prepared, lay it on the countertop while you grease the bowl with a fine layer of oil. Next, turn the dough in the oil several times so that the dough is greased lightly on all sides.

6   Cover the bowl with a large plastic garbage bag or kitchen towel and allow it to rise for 1 hour.

7   Make the blessing on *hafrashat challah* — see **Hafrashat Challah, page 17.**

8   Knead the dough again for a few more minutes and then divide the dough into 12 equal parts and knead into balls. Use the remaining flour for surface area and hands to prevent sticking.

9   With a rolling pin, flatten balls. With a knife cut each piece into the shape of a flame.

10   Indent lines into the bottom section of the 'flame', to create definition to the flame. If there is any remaining dough from all the cuts, combine all the remnants to make another flame.

11   Cover the loaves again and let them rise in a warm place for 1 hour or until the dough has doubled in volume from its original size. You may need to go over the lines again if they rose up.

12   If you cannot bake the challahs immediately, then this is the time to wrap the shaped dough in plastic wrap to prevent drying. You can store it in the coldest part of the refrigerator for up to 48 hours. On the day of baking, remove the dough from refrigerator and let stand on kitchen counter until it comes to room temperature, about one hour.

13   Preheat the oven to 350° F (180° C). Glaze with egg wash and sprinkle with corn grits.

14 Bake in your preheated oven for about 25-30 minutes, or until loaves turn golden brown and shiny. Bread should have a nice hollow sound when thumped on the bottom.

15 Remove from the oven and cool on a rack. Wait at least one hour before serving. If you are freezing the challah, wrap in waxed paper and foil. It can be stored in the freezer for up to 2 months.

Introduction to Challah Theme during the Yeast Activation

Rededication

The month of Kislev is all about Chanukah. Antiochus IV Epiphanes was the king of the Seleucid Empire, which included the province of Judea, during the second century B.C.E. The Seleucids were Hellenists, proponents of Classical Greek culture. Antiochus decided to outlaw Jewish traditions, ordering the worship of Zeus, and desecrating the Temple. The Maccabees led the Jewish rebellion against this outrage, and were successful in ridding the land of the Seleucids and gaining autonomy for the Jewish people for the first time in centuries. The eight-day festival of Chanukah commemorates the rededication of the Temple after the rebellion succeeded.

The first act of purifying the Holy Temple entailed relighting the menorah, the "lamp of God,"[1] which was supposed to burn continuously in the Temple. The light served as testimony to the world that the Divine presence rested in Israel.[2] Searching the plundered and defiled Temple, the Maccabees found one last flask of olive oil bearing the seal of the high priest, Yochanan. The flask only contained enough oil to last one day, but miraculously, the oil burned for eight days — enough time for the Maccabees to prepare a fresh supply. The Chanukah miracle teaches us how effort and miracle go hand in hand. The miracle of the oil burning for eight days didn't happen until the Maccabees had fought for their beliefs, and had exerted the effort of searching for a flask of pure olive oil with which to light the menorah.

To mark and celebrate this miracle, we light candles for eight days, and the Chanukah menorahs (or Chanukiahs) are placed in the doorways or windows of our homes so that the light can illuminate not just our homes but our streets, piercing the darkness and publically acknowledging the miracle. Along with lighting a Chanukiah every night, we also commemorate the miracle of the oil by eating foods fried in olive oil. We are using olive oil in our challah to extend this idea. Olive oil can also represent the strength and persistence of the Jewish people. The oil is only extracted from the olive through squeezing and compressing it, and then straining the oil to remove impurities. Much like the Jews, who, through oppression, rise and prevail.

During the Middle Ages, a *piyyut* (Jewish liturgical poem) telling a variation of the story of Judith was customarily sung on the Shabbat of Chanukah.[3] The *piyyut* was based on *midrashim* that connect the story of Judith[4] with the story of Chanukah. Judith is described as the daughter of the high priest, Yochanan. She charmed her way into the tent of one of the Seleucid generals, and plied him with salty cheese so that he would be thirsty enough to drink lots of wine. He became so drunk that he fell into a stupor, at which point she beheaded him. This story is the source for the custom of eating cheese foods on Chanukah.[5] We will be making cheese challah in honor of Judith's courage. If you are preparing a meat meal for Shabbat, then you can forgo the dairy challah and instead make a pareve challah shaped into a flame,

---

1   Samuel 3:3

2   Babylonian Talmud, Shabbat 22b

3   The twelfth-century piyyut was titled "Mi Kamocha Adir Ayom Ve-Nora" ("Who is like You [God], mighty, awesome and terrible").

4   The Book of Judith was not included in the Jewish Bible, but is an ancient story included in the Septuagint and the Christian 'Old Testament.'

5   Nissim ben Reuben (ca. 1310–75), known as the Ran, refers to Judith not by name, but as the daughter of Yochanan. In his account, which he says comes from a midrash (Shabbat 10a on Babylonian Talmud Shabbat 23b), the woman gave the chief enemy cheese to eat so as to make him drunk, and then cut off his head. This, adds the Ran, is why it is customary to eat cheese on Chanukah.

to echo the lights on the Chanukiah. The flame surges upwards towards the energy of the heavens. Our job on this earth is to light the world with the wisdom of Torah.

Meditation during Kneading

Chanukah celebrates our redemption from foreign powers that attempted to persuade us to abandon God and Torah. The Chanukah lights spark holiness in realms of darkness. The Hebrew word *Chanukah*, dedication, shares the same root as the word *chinuch*, education. We are the lights of Chanukah and we must educate the world through the light of Torah. We will meditate on building our inner light, which is our Divine light. There is no darkness or concealment in this Divine light, only truth. When you experience that Divine light as love from God, it has the ability to burst outwards into the physical act of kneading. That is an ideal way to experience God — His love is so enrapturing that we feel the urge to express it through His *mitzvot*, thereby sharing the light of Torah.

- Start with gentle belly breathing from the nose. This allows you to have more control over your breath. Slowly inhale and exhale, pulling your breath all the way into your belly. Feel your belly expand.

- Be totally present. If your mind wanders, calmly bring it back.

- Envision a stairway rising before you, with a bright light at the top. You want to reach that light. It beckons you.

- There are eight steps for you to climb. Slowly ascend them. With each step, allow the light to fill you — showering you from your crown as it washes over your entire body, capturing every cell in your body.

- Feel this light as a thrust of energy that needs to be released through your hands.

- Knead this energy, this love, into the dough.

After the meditation is complete, smell a fragrant spice such as cloves to re-involve yourself with the physical world and help you feel grounded again.

Discussion during the Rising

Chanukah Heroism Lights Up the Darkness

It is not clear whether the *Book of Judith* was originally written in Hebrew or in Greek. The oldest version extant is found in the *Septuagint,* a Greek translation of the Bible,[6] while the Hebrew version dates back to medieval times. Although the two versions contradict each other in many details, their commonality is the woman, Judith, who beheaded a general. According to the medieval Hebrew version, Judith's story took place during the time of the Maccabean revolt.

Judith was from the town of Bethulia, which was under siege by Holofernes — a mighty Seleucid general — at the head of a huge army.

At the time, Antiochus IV was in control of Judea, and was oppressing the Jews. He had placed a Hellenistic priest in the Holy Temple and required the sacrifice of pigs on its altar. Thousands of Jews had been massacred, and vital religious practices had been banned, including circumcision, Rosh Chodesh and Shabbat: "And the king

---

6 The Septuagint is the earliest extant Greek translation of the Pentateuch from the original Hebrew, dating from the 3rd century BCE. The name is derived from the legend that there were seventy-two translators, six from each of the twelve tribes, each working in separate cells, who all produced identical translations.

sent letters by messengers to Jerusalem and the cities of Judah; he directed them to follow customs strange to the land, to forbid burnt offerings and sacrifices and drink offerings in the Sanctuary, to profane sabbaths and feasts, to defile the Sanctuary and the priests, to build altars and sacred precincts and shrines for idols, to sacrifice swine and unclean animals, and to leave their sons uncircumcised. They were to make themselves abominable by everything unclean and profane, so that they should forget the law and change all the ordinances." [7]

Antiochus wanted the Jews to assimilate totally into Hellenist culture. By interfering with Jewish rituals, they aimed to sever the Jews' connection to their spiritual underpinnings. Many of the most cherished ideas in Judaism ran counter to the Hellenist ideal. The Greek aesthetic idolized the human form and repudiated the idea of bodily imperfection or restraint, so they found the idea of circumcision abhorrent. The idea of one day a week being dedicated to spiritual pleasure through material withdrawal was likewise repugnant. At that time, Hellenistic culture dominated the known world, and was a center of great creativity. The idea of taking one day to let God run the world negated the Greek belief in the ultimate power of the individual. And finally, by banning Rosh Chodesh, Jews would not know when to celebrate any of their holy days and the sacred cycle of the year would fail.

Two major groups opposed Antiochus: a group led by Matityahu the Hasmonean with his son Judah Maccabee, and a fiercely religious sect known as the Hasideans (no direct connection to the modern movement known as Chasidism). They joined forces to revolt against not only the oppression of the Seleucid Greek government, but also the assimilation of those Jews who were attracted to the Hellenist ideas of their rulers.

Holofernes was determined to crush the rebellion in the town of Bethulia, whose inhabitants refused to recognize the oppressive rule of the Seleucids. He cut off their food and water supply, and before long the town was brought to near surrender — until Judith came up with a plan.

Judith, a pious widow who was blessed with extraordinary wit, charm and grace, beseeched Uzziah, one of the leaders of Bethulia, to give her permission to leave the town, with her maid, for a personal visit with Holofernes. Judith was granted permission and left for Holofernes' encampment with her faithful maid, who carried on her head a basket filled with homemade rolls, cheeses and several bottles of fine wine.

Judith convinced the guardsmen to let them enter the camp and meet Holofernes by informing them she had a plan as to how he could capture the town without losing any men. When Holofernes met Judith, he was completely captivated, and invited her to dine with him. He was hoping to bed her, but she had other plans.

Judith entered Holofernes' tent with the delicacies she had brought with her and fed him salty cheese, chunk after chunk, which he washed down with wine. Before long he was sprawled on the ground, dead drunk. A play on words.

Judith unsheathed Holofernes' heavy sword and, taking aim at his neck, she brought the sword down with all her might and beheaded him. She wrapped the general's head in rags, concealed it under her shawl, and calmly walked out.

She then returned to Uzziah and told him to prepare Bethulia's defenders for a surprise attack on the Seleucids, at dawn the next day. When Holofernes' soldiers found his corpse, they were overcome with fear; the Jews, on the other hand, had been emboldened, and launched a successful attack. The town was saved, and the Seleucid

---

7   Maccabees I 1:41-49

army was defeated due to Judith's courageous act. The story of Judith exemplifies the Chanukah theme of Jewish faith and courage overcoming a larger force.

Judah Maccabee instituted the celebration of Chanukah in 165 B.C.E. to celebrate and mark the rededication of the Temple after a dark time. Chanukah begins four days before the new moon, when the moon is scarcely visible — it is the darkest night of the month. Moreover, Chanukah falls close to the winter solstice — a time of year with the shortest days and longest nights; days are so short that there can be as little as ten hours of daylight. It seems only natural that a key theme of this holiday is lighting darkness. Lighting darkness can also be viewed in a more metaphorical way, as a reminder of those Jews who lost their way during the Hellenist period. Every night of Chanukah, an extra candle is lit, increasing the intensity of the light night by night, publically illuminating awareness of the one God and His Torah.

Judaism sees fire as a vehicle to connect us to something higher. Every Shabbat and festival demands the lighting of candles. At the moment immediately preceding the beginning of the auspicious day, the tradition is to light one or more candles. Shabbat candles are lit for the purpose of *kavod*, honor, to pay tribute to the day, and also for the purpose of oneg, pleasure, and *shalom bayit*, harmony in the home, so that we may eat our Shabbat meal in their pleasing glow. On festivals, we mark the additional element of a day of simcha, a day of joy. The flame of a candle is often seen as representing the soul, so we also light a candle when remembering a departed relative on the day of their *yahrzeit* (anniversary of the day of death of a relative).[8]

The lights of Chanukah are actually not meant to be used for our personal pleasure whatsoever, unlike the lights of Shabbat and other festivals. The *shamash* (assistant) candle is present on the Chanukiah to *prevent* use of the candles for anything other than publicizing and reflecting on the miracle of Chanukah — if other lights were to go out, then we 'use' the light of the *shamash* to see by, thus avoiding using the other candles. Reflecting on the miracle of Chanukah, the kindled candles can remind us of our purpose in life — bringing light into the dark corners of the world.

The ability to bring light into dark corners is contingent upon two elements: the existence of light itself, and an empty space for it to illuminate. As the Kabbalah teaches, the more empty the vessel, the greater its capacity to receive.[9]

When the moon is a mere sliver in the sky and we seem to be surrounded by darkness, lighting candles can remind us of our purpose in life — bringing light into the dark corners of the world, illuminating the empty spaces. We each have the power to bring light into the world with every decision, action, thought and word. When faced with darkness, we should remember Judith, a Jewish woman who took matters into her own hands and courageously found a way to help save her people, her religion and her land. The story of this brave Jewish woman teaches us that living as a Jew is something that often requires courage, self-sacrifice and dedication. When the Maccabees retrieved control of the Holy Temple and restored Jewish independence, they also reclaimed our religious traditions, including Rosh Chodesh, on which we are baking these challahs, and Shabbat, when we will eat them.

---

8 This connection derives from the verse in Proverbs, "The soul of man is the candle of God" (20:27).

9 According to the Arizal, Rabbi Yitzchak Luria, God began the process of creation by 'contracting' his infinite light in order to allow for an unoccupied 'space' in which the world could exist and be independent. This doctrine is known as tzimtzum — contraction. Without tzimtzum there would be no room for humans to have free will. Therefore, paradoxically, the removal of God's light allowed humanity to begin the process of unification with God — filling the world with light through the study of Torah and adherence to God's commandments.

Reflective Questions

1. What kind of resistance did Judith exhibit?

2. What was Judith fighting for? Could you have done the same? What other methods would you employ?

3. What is Chanukah really about? How does this differ from the popular celebrations of today? Why do you think the celebration has changed over the course of time?

4. If the Jews were fighting Hellenism during the Maccabean revolt, do you think Chanukah gifts are appropriate?

5. The Chanukah festival lasts eight days. What other festivals/milestones are eight days? What significance does the number eight have? Are there any correlations amongst any of these festivals or milestones that are eight days?

6. To what might you rededicate yourself now?

7. What is Chanukah about for you?

8. What light can we create?

9. How do you define a miracle?

10. How do we make Chanukah's light our own personal inner light?

Kavanah for Hafrashat Challah

On the Chanukiah, the *shamash* candle is used solely to light the other candles. The *shamash* is differentiated from the rest of the candles by being placed separately, either above or below the other candles. You are the *shamash* candle — differentiated from the rest and used to educate the world with Torah. Focus on one way you can serve as a *shamash*.

The procedure and blessing for the *hafrashat challah* ceremony can be found on pages 14-17. Participants may wish to shape the challah afterwards, or take it home and shape it there.

Star of David Challah (Egg Challah)

Yields: 6 Stars

INGREDIENTS

4 tablespoons active dry yeast

4 ½ cups (1.1 liters) warm water

¾ cup (150 g) organic sugar plus 2 tablespoons
organic sugar

5 pounds (2.25 kg) organic white flour

1 ½ tablespoons sea salt

1 cup (230 ml) neutral-tasting oil, such as
safflower oil

Topping

2 cage-free organic eggs, beaten
Coarse Sea salt

1   In a large bowl, combine the yeast with the 2 tablespoons of sugar and the warm water. Cover the bowl and allow the mixture to start activating. Yeast activation should take about 10 minutes; it will be bubbling and foamy.

2   Set 1 cup (125 g) of flour aside. Sift the remaining flour, sugar, and salt into a large bowl.

3   Pour the yeast mixture and oil onto the flour. Combine all the ingredients, using a spatula. When it begins to form a dough, it is time to knead. At this point, you can remove the dough from the bowl and knead on the kitchen counter if it's easier for you, or directly in the bowl.

4   To knead the dough: grab the side of the dough furthest away from you and fold it toward yourself. Fold the dough in half and use your body weight to push the dough into itself. If you find that the dough is sticking too much to the surface and preventing you from kneading properly, dust the dough with flour. Give the dough a quarter turn (90 degrees). Grab the other side and fold it in half. Again, with a lot of weight behind it, push the newly folded half into itself. Repeat this process for 10-15 minutes or until the dough is smooth, silky, elastic and the dough does not stick to the surface.

5   After the dough is thoroughly prepared, lay it on the countertop while you grease the bowl with a fine layer of oil. Next, turn the dough in the oil several times so that the dough is greased lightly on all sides.

6   Cover the bowl with a large plastic garbage bag or kitchen towel and allow it to rise for 1 hour.

7   Make the blessing on *hafrashat challah* — see **Hafrashat Challah, page 17.**

8   Knead the dough again for a few more minutes and then divide the dough into 16 equal parts. Use the remaining flour to flour the surface area and hands to prevent sticking.

9   Roll each out into a strand of about 10 inches (25 cm) long and 1 inch (2.5 cm) in diameter

10 Line a baking sheet with parchment paper. Lay 3 strands on the prepared baking sheet in a triangle shape, and pinch together firmly at the ends. Weave 3 more strands over and underneath each point of the first triangle to make a second, interwoven triangle. Pinch it closed tightly at the edges to make a six-pointed star.

11 Set the baking sheet in a warm place and allow to rise for 30 minutes. Pinch the seams again firmly in place, so it does not open during baking. If you cannot bake the challahs immediately, then this is the time to wrap the shaped dough in plastic wrap to prevent drying. You can store it in the coldest part of the refrigerator for up to 48 hours. On the day of baking, remove the dough from the refrigerator and let stand on kitchen counter until it comes to room temperature, about one hour.

12 Preheat the oven to 350° F (180° C). Glaze the stars with egg wash and then sprinkle coarse sea salt on the top for decoration.

13 Bake in your preheated oven for about 30-35 minutes, or until loaves turn golden brown and shiny. Bread should have a nice hollow sound when thumped on the bottom.

14 Remove from the oven and cool on a rack. Wait at least one hour before serving. If you are freezing the challah, wrap in waxed paper and foil. It can be stored in the freezer for up to 2 months.

Before Preparing the Dough, recite optional Rosh Chodesh Psalms, page 19.

Mourning and Consolation

Some 2,500 years ago, on the tenth of Tevet, the armies of the Babylonian emperor Nebuchadnezzar laid siege to the city of Jerusalem. This was the first in a series of events that ultimately led to the destruction of the Holy Temple and the exile of the Jewish people from the Land of Israel. The events that followed — the breaching of the city's walls during the month of Tammuz, and the destruction of the First Temple three-and-a-half years later, on Tisha B'Av — could not have taken place had the city not been besieged in the first place. Thus the Tenth of Tevet was decreed to be a day of fasting and repentance, on which we mourn these tragic events, contemplate their deeper causes and work to correct similar issues in our own souls and deeds.

The path to destruction and exile began long before the siege of Jerusalem, when the Jews began straying from God by worshipping idols.[1] Four hundred years after the Jews settled in the Land of Israel, their relationship with God was consummated with the completion and dedication of the Holy Temple in Jerusalem. The Temple was supposed to stand forever, as long as the Jews adhered to God's Torah. Initially, under King Solomon's[2] reign, the Jews followed God's commandments and were steadfast in their faith, thus enjoying peace, prosperity and a direct connection to God through His Temple. However, toward the end of King Solomon's life, he began to worship the gods of his foreign wives. As a

result, God told him that his kingdom would be wrested away from his son. [3]

After King Solomon's death, just as God had warned, the ten northern tribes refused to accept his son, Rehoboam, as their king. Subsequently, the country divided into two kingdoms: the Kingdom of Israel in the north, of ten tribes, and the Kingdom of Judah, including Jerusalem, in the south, which consisted of two tribes: Judah and Benjamin, plus the Levites.[4] The two kingdoms were perpetually at war with each other, and in both the practice of idolatry became widespread despite repeated reprimands from prophets such as Jeremiah, who warned them that the Temple would be destroyed if they did not repent.[5] Ultimately, God punished the Jews for deserting Him by allowing the destruction of the First Temple in 586 BCE, and consequently the first exile of the Jews, to Babylonia — an exile that even today has not quite ended.

Two of the ingredients in our regular challah recipe carry allusions to this month's theme: eggs and salt. In Judaism, the egg is traditionally seen as a symbol of both mourning and consolation. Mourners eat eggs during

---

1   The Babylonian Talmud, Yoma 9b, states that the First Temple was destroyed because of three things; idolatry, immoral sexual practices and murder.

2   King Solomon was the son of King David, and reigned from approximately 970 to 931 BCE.

3   Kings I, 11:9-13. God was angry with Solomon, because his heart had turned away from God, who had appeared to him twice and had commanded him not go after other gods. But he did not keep what God commanded. Therefore God said to Solomon, "Since this has been your practice and you have not kept my covenant and my statutes that I have commanded you, I will surely tear the kingdom from you and will give it to your servant. Yet for the sake of David your father I will not do it in your days, but I will tear it out of the hand of your son. However, I will not tear away all the kingdom, but I will give one tribe to your son, for the sake of David my servant and for the sake of Jerusalem that I have chosen."

4   The tribe of Levi was not given an allotment of land like the other tribes, because they served as priests for the entire nation. Instead they were given forty-eight cities, scattered throughout the land. When the kingdom divided, the Levites left those cities that were in the Northern kingdom and went to the Southern kingdom.

5   Book of Lamentations ("Eichah")

the first meal after a burial, and eggs are also eaten at the last meal before the Fast of Tisha B'Av. The shape of an egg, as well as its function, remind us of the wheel of life, forever turning, bringing both death and life. Even in the face of death, danger and destruction, we must remain hopeful of all the promise that a new life can bring. Although we grieve because we are presently without the Temple, we may take comfort in the hope that coming together in a Rosh Chodesh group, united, is one way to atone for the divisions of our ancestors.

Salt is symbolic of both mourning and consolation. Traditionally, salt is a sign of sadness, because it is reminiscent of tears. When we cry, we are also purifying ourselves, purging via salty tears. Similarly, salt is used to kosher meat, purging it of blood, which cannot be consumed. After reciting the blessing over bread, we sprinkle salt over it to symbolize the salt that was once sprinkled over the sacrifices in the Temple, symbolic of our everlasting covenant with God. Thus when you use salt, you are both purifying and consecrating for holiness.

We will shape the challahs as "Stars of David." In Psalm 18, King David called God a shield: "God's way is perfect; the word of the Lord is flawless; He is a shield to all who trust in Him" (18:31). A shield is a piece of armor that is held in front of the body to protect it from sword strokes or falling arrows. King David's description ultimately became connected with the hexagram, a compound of two equilateral triangles that has come to be identified with Jews and Judaism, as the *Star of David.* This shape serves to remind us that we can never let our enemies breach our relationship with God. Adding salt flakes to the top of the challah is a mournful reminder that due to the destruction of the Temple, we can no longer offer sacrifices, which would have been sprinkled with salt.

Meditation during Kneading

Since the tenth of Tevet is the day when the armies of King Nebuchadnezzar laid siege to the walls of Jerusalem, we observe it as a day of fasting and repentance — a day devoted to shielding the walls of our Jewish identity and repairing its breaches. This meditation is about protecting our connection with God from any breaches that would sever us from our one and only Source.

We will do a mantra meditation in which we address God as our shield — *Hashem hu HaMagen.* We will strive to feel God right in front of us, protecting us — our divine armor.

- Start with gentle belly breathing from the nose. This allows you to have more control over your breath. Slowly inhale and exhale, pulling your breath all the way into your belly. Feel your belly expand.

- Be totally present as you inhale and exhale. If your mind wanders, calmly bring it back.

- Continue to focus on your breath, and just your breath. Feel the difference in temperature between how the air goes in and how it goes out.

- Once you feel yourself enter a meditative state, direct your thoughts to the verse, *Hashem hu HaMagen,* God is the Shield.

- Keep repeating the words. You may say the mantra aloud or in your head, but you must repeat it to yourself throughout the knead.

- Concentrate on the meaning of the verse, allowing its spiritual power to filter through your mind and heart as it travels via your kneading hands to the dough.

- Feel God as your shield, right in front of you. Feel the grandeur of His great power surrounding you on all sides. Become aware of His closeness, shielding you from harm.

- Let your enthusiasm for and commitment to the *mitzvah* you are performing through this act of kneading be your shield and protection.

After the meditation is complete, smell a fragrant spice such as cloves to re-involve yourself with the physical world and make you feel grounded again. Whenever you feel that your relationship with God is in jeopardy, you can always access this shield. He is always there for you.

Discussion during the Rising

Protecting our Walls

The peoples of the Ancient Middle East were, above all else, highly superstitious, erecting idols to represent their many gods and worshipping both the gods and the idols directly. This conflicted with the monotheism espoused in the Torah. Monotheism rejects the belief that there can be more than one God that any created thing might have power independent of God, or that anything can be a mediator between people and God. Many Jews went against the Torah by accepting the existence and power of other peoples' gods. They would adopt a local god or gods into their worship as a cultic practice. When large segments of the Jewish people succumbed to idolatry, they were succumbing to the sin of living without responsibility toward or faith in the Highest Authority. They breached their relationship with God. The prophet Jeremiah warned the people again and again that they

must stop their worship of idols and their mistreatment of each other. At that time, the kingdom of Judah was a vassal state of Babylon, and paid a yearly tribute to the ancient superpower. Jeremiah warned the king, and the people, that God would bring down the wrath of Babylon upon them to destroy them, but they refused to listen to him. Eventually, events fell out as he had foretold.

The saga of persecution began on the tenth of Tevet, 588 BCE. Nebuchadnezzar, the king of Babylon, had attempted an invasion of Egypt that ended in failure, and this emboldened several states to rebel against Babylonian control. The kingdom of Judah stopped paying tribute, believing the Babylonians had become too weak to respond. This enraged Nebuchadnezzar, who regrouped his forces and began to reassert his control over the Middle Eastern regions.

Jerusalem was surrounded by Babylonian forces in a siege that lasted for eighteen months: "And it was in the ninth year of his reign, in the tenth month,[6] in the tenth (day) of the month, that Nebuchadnezzar, King of Babylon came, he and all his host, upon Jerusalem, and he encamped against it and built a siege wall around it. And the city was besieged until the eleventh year of King Tzidkiyahu. And on the ninth day of the fourth month famine was intense in the city, the people had no bread, and the city was breached" (Kings II 5:1-4). Three weeks after the walls were breached, the First Temple was destroyed.

According to the Talmud, the Temple was rebuilt seventy years later because the Jews had repented of their sins. The Second Temple was destroyed approximately six hundred years later because of causeless hatred. Today,

---

6   Nisan is the 'first month' according to Exodus, therefore the tenth month is Tevet.

two thousand years later, it has still not been rebuilt, as the people have not repented to the extent that we merit it.[7] How can we be worthy again? Through the correction of the transgressions that caused the destruction of the Second Temple. "Every generation in whose days the Sanctuary is not built, it is reckoned unto them, as though they had destroyed it."[8] This statement in the Talmud asserts that every generation *has* the capacity, and therefore the responsibility, to awaken God's mercy, in order for Israel to be redeemed, by way of the Messiah. Then, the final Temple will be rebuilt.

Although the fast on the tenth of Tevet is observed as a sad day, we can also view this day as an opportune day. As the moon pushes outwards, we should fold inwards into a contemplative state, asking ourselves questions like: why did the Sages institute a fast day when the walls were merely breached in Jerusalem,[9] while the Temple was not even destroyed yet? Are there fences that we need to set in place to ensure that our relationship with God will not be compromised? What is the root for the baseless hatred that must still exist between Jews, since we have not been redeemed yet? What thoughts, actions and intentions do we need to put into place — permanently — so that we may merit in the rebuilding of the Third Temple and finally find ourselves living with peace and clarity?[10]

One of the ways we can make restitution is by gathering together on Rosh Chodesh, honoring the traditional link between Jewish women and the banishing of idolatry. The celebration and observance of Rosh Chodesh was given specifically to Jewish women as a reward for not having been willing to participate in the sin of the Golden Calf. When Moses did not descend from Mount Sinai when the people expected him to, it was the women who did not lose faith amidst the cold darkness of the desert, but held to the steadfast faith that God could not have possibly abandoned them. Within the darkness is where they found their inner light, and shielded their relationship with God.

Another way we can actively reject the idea of idolatry, thereby bringing *tikkun* (repair) to the world, is by fulfilling the commandment of performing *hafrashat challah*, separating the dough. This memorializes the tithing of bread to the priests who were working in the Temple. Although we don't have the Temple anymore, we still separate a portion of the dough to commemorate the interdependence between the *kohanim* and the Israelites. Today, instead of tithing this portion, we burn it as a holy consecration to God. By doing this, we are recognizing that it is really He that gives us our "bread." We acknowledge that God is the ultimate giver.

Every Jewish home has the potential to be a microcosm of the Temple, so the work that women do in making challah is literally holy work. Our physical act, today, of baking challah, affirms our connection to God, demonstrating that we intend to reject any form of idolatry. Our mantra today has placed God front and center in our lives. Moreover, gathering together within a Rosh Chodesh cohort of women empowers us with the realization that we are all in this together! Despite our differences, despite any animosities and quarrels that might drive us apart, we know that we share a common fate, a common identity, and a common goal — to bring divinity into this world. Our collective *tikkun*, our redemption, will only come if we are unified, and show unconditional love for each other.

---

7   Babylonian Talmud, Yoma 9b

8   Jerusalem Talmud, Yoma 1:1

9   2 Kings 25:1 and Ezekiel 24:1-14

10 This period of peace and clarity is referred to as the Messianic Age, which will be characterized by the peaceful co-existence of all people (Isaiah 2: 2-4). Hatred, intolerance and war will cease to exist. Even the laws of nature will change, so that predatory beasts will no longer seek prey, and agriculture will bring forth super-natural abundance (Isaiah 11:6-11:9), although some sages believe this to be an allegory for peace and prosperity.

The fast of the Tenth of Tevet is observed only a week after the festival of Chanukah ends. A week after we finish celebrating and commemorating the rededication of the Holy Temple, we spend a day mourning the siege of Jerusalem; a siege that ultimately led to the destruction of the Temple. This is an extreme transition, going from the holiday of lights, of spiritual miracles, to a day of national darkness and fasting. Although there is no direct correlation between the two events occurring so close together, I think there might be an underlying message for us to ponder. The lights that we lit for Chanukah have been integrated within us, so that *we* become the guiding light for hope and redemption. In fact, the meditation last month was about building and sustaining our own inner light, so that nothing can sever our relationship with God. Carrying the light of redemption into the darkness of destruction can help us focus on the way forward, the promise that we *are* capable of bringing redemption if we try hard enough.

We may be surrounded by enemy forces that continually try to breach our walls and sever our connection to our Torah, our Land, and our God, yet we still resist, just as the Maccabees did. Ultimately, we will prevail by continuing to stand against those who seek to diminish the Divine light in this world.

Reflective Questions

1. Do you have any superstitions? Do you do any practices to ward them off? How do these superstitions serve you? Where did you learn of these superstitions?

2. Do you think God acted harshly when He destroyed the Temple because of the Jews' behavior?

3. Today, most Jews don't practice the ancient form of idolatry. What do you consider a modern form of idolatry? Ultimately how might it affect your relationship with God?

4. Does the modern form of idolatry fulfill any needs? What might they be?

5. King Solomon was considered one of the wisest men in Judaism, and yet he still succumbed to idolatry towards the end of his life. Is there a practice you could include in your life, forever, that would prevent a breach with God?

6. How does protecting your relationship with God, also protect your relationship with your fellow wo/man? Is there even a correlation?

Kavanah for Hafrashat Challah

Ask God to shield you and your family from any temptations that would breach your relationship with Him, that you may play your part in *tikkun olam* by infusing the world with spirituality and the Divine.

The procedure and blessing for the *hafrashat challah* ceremony can be found on pages 14-17. Participants may wish to shape the challah afterwards, or take it home and shape it there.

SHVAT

NOTE: For this month's challah it is preferable to use ingredients that are from Israel.

Seven Species Pomegranate-shaped Challah*

Yields: 6 challahs

Ingredients

4 tablespoons active dry yeast

2 tablespoons organic sugar

4 ½ cups (1.1 liters) warm water

5 pounds (2.25 kg) organic white flour

One 12-ounce (350 g) container of date honey (silan)**

1 ½ tablespoons sea salt

1 cup (230 ml) olive oil

1 cup (150 g) finely-diced dried figs

1 cup (150 g) raisins

Topping

2 cage-free organic eggs, beaten

2 tablespoons pomegranate syrup, in egg wash

Barley grits

---

* This original design was inspired by Amanda of The Challah Blog: http://www.thechallahblog.com/2012/08/rosh-hashanah-challah-shape-pomegranate.html

** Silan can be purchased in most kosher supermarkets and Mediterranean food markets.

1. In a large bowl, combine the yeast with the 2 tablespoons of sugar and the warm water. Cover the bowl and allow the mixture to start activating. Yeast activation should take about 10 minutes; it will be bubbling and foamy.

2. Set 1 cup (125 g) of flour aside. Sift the remaining flour, and salt into the bowl.

3. To knead the dough: grab the side of the dough furthest away from you and fold it toward yourself. Fold the dough in half and use your body weight to push the dough into itself. If you find that the dough is sticking too much to the surface and preventing you from kneading properly, dust the dough with flour. Give the dough a quarter turn (90 degrees). Grab the other side and fold it in half. Again, with a lot of weight behind it, push the newly folded half into itself. Repeat this process for 10-15 minutes, or until the dough is smooth, silky, elastic and the dough does not stick to the surface.

4. After the dough is thoroughly prepared, lay it on the countertop while you grease the bowl with a fine layer of oil. Next, turn the dough in the oil several times so that the dough is greased lightly on all sides.

5. Cover the bowl with a large plastic garbage bag or kitchen towel and allow it to rise for 1 hour.

6. Make the blessing on *hafrashat challah* — see **Hafrashat Challah, page 17.**

7   Knead the dried figs and raisins into the dough for a few more minutes and then divide dough into 12 equal parts. Use the remaining flour to flour surface area and hands to prevent sticking.

8   With a rolling pin, roll out 6 of the balls into nice smooth strands — as long as you can, and then continue to extend the strands with your palms, out *really long* — about 4 feet (1.2 m). This will form the "frame" of your pomegranate.

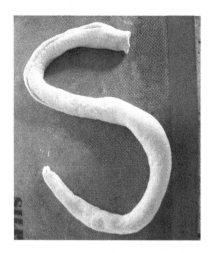

9   On a piece of parchment paper that has been placed on a greased baking sheet, shape the long strand into an S-shape.

10   Roll out the rest of your dough (the remaining 6 logs) and cut them into 1-inch (2.5 cm) size pieces. Roll each piece in your palms, into the size of a golf-ball. You will use these as pomegranate "seeds."

11   Place about eight "seed" dough balls into the lower half of the S. This will form the body of your pomegranate. Then take the upper half of the S and reshape it into the top of the pomegranate, in a zigzag, making sure to pinch the ends closed.

12   Repeat with the other strands and balls to form the other five pomegranate challahs.

13   Don't let this challah rise as long as you normally would, as it would completely lose its shape. Limit the second rise to just 15 minutes. Pinch the ends again before glazing the challah with egg-wash.

14   If you cannot bake the challahs immediately, then this is the time to wrap the shaped dough in plastic wrap to prevent drying. You can store it in the coldest part of the refrigerator for up to 48 hours. On the day of baking, remove the dough from refrigerator and let stand on kitchen counter until it comes to room temperature, about one hour.

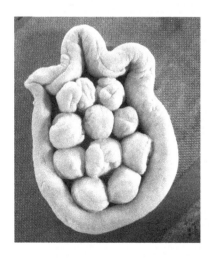

16 Preheat the oven to 350° F (180° C). Mix the beaten eggs with the pomegranate syrup. Brush your challahs with beaten eggs and sprinkle with barley grits.

17 Bake in your preheated oven for about 30-35 minutes, or until loaves turn golden brown and shiny. Bread should have a nice hollow sound when thumped on the bottom.

18 Remove from the oven and cool on a rack. Wait at least one hour before serving. If you are freezing the challah, wrap in waxed paper and foil. It can be stored in the freezer for up to 2 months.

Before Preparing the Dough, recite optional *Rosh Chodesh Psalms, page 19.*

Insights from the Seven Species Challah

Although in many parts of the world it is still winter, Tu B'Shvat — the fifteenth of Shvat, the New Year of the Trees, also known as *Chag Ha'Ilanot* — foretells the coming of spring and presents an opportunity to honor the forthcoming season with a heightened *taste*.[1] Tu B'Shvat is listed in the *Mishna* (oral law) as the date used for calculating the beginning of the agricultural cycle for the purpose of biblical tithes. Today, it offers us a unique opportunity for insight into our personal growth through an exploration of the connection between trees, their fruits and our spiritual existence. Throughout the centuries, kabbalists have used the tree as a metaphor to understand God's relationship to the spiritual and physical worlds.[2]

In the 16th century, the kabbalists of Safed compiled a Tu B'Shvat *seder*, modeled to a certain degree on the Pesach *seder*. It included readings from the Torah, Talmud (oral law with accompanying commentary) and Zohar (mystical commentary on the Torah), with special blessings to be said over fruits and fruit-bearing trees. Four cups of wine were also drunk.

The *seder* placed special emphasis on Shivat Haminim — the Seven Species of produce native to the Land of Israel which are mentioned in the Torah: wheat, barley, grapes, figs, pomegranates, olives and honey.[3] When God promised the land of Israel to the Jewish people, He mentioned these seven species by name to prove the land's viability, as these grains and fruits were staples in their diet. This suggests that God invoked divinity into each one of these species.[4] When we eat from any one of these, we should be mindful that we are ingesting holy sparks into our lives as a conduit to reach God, which is also why we need to say a blessing to Him for this gift. We will be using all of these fruits in our challah preparation, to honor Tu B'Shvat, and to re-engage our taste for the new fruits by elevating them with intention.

With this in mind, Shvat can be viewed as a month of holy eating. It is a chance to understand God in the most basic, primal and intimate way, by connecting through the eating of the seven blessed species.

Wheat was mentioned first in the seven species because it is the foundation of sustenance. It was considered superior to barley because it was a finer grain, more suitable for human consumption. During biblical times, the choicest wheat was used in meal offerings. While wheat may have been essential for life, the Torah emphasizes "man does not live by bread alone, by the utterance of God's mouth does man live" (Deuteronomy 8:3). In other words, it is not just our earthly toils that bring us "bread" but the blessings from above which endow our efforts with success. In order for us to draw down blessings, we have to be involved in our own

---

1 According to the Sefer Yetzirah, the sense connected with Shevat is 'Le'itah', taste. "Ta'amu ure'u ki tov Hashem,"— "Taste and see that God is good." (Psalms 34:9)

2 Moshe Chaim Luzzatto, known as The Ramchal, in his 18th century classic, *The Way of God*, teaches that the higher spiritual realms are "roots" that ultimately manifest their influence through "branches and leaves" in the lower realms.

3 Deuteronomy 8:8. The honey referred to comes from dates, not bees.

4 The blessing Bracha Achat Me'ein Shalosh is recited after eating grains, or wine, or any of the five fruits that belong within the Seven Species — grapes, figs, pomegranates, olives and dates. It differs from the blessing said after any other fruits in its gracious praise of the land of Israel and its fruits: "Blessed are You, Lord our God, King of the universe, for the tree and the fruit of the tree, for the produce of the field, and for the precious, good and spacious land which You have graciously given as a heritage to our ancestors, to eat of its fruit and be satiated with its goodness… For You, Lord, are good and do good to all, and we will thank You for the land and for her fruits. Blessed are You Lord, for the land and for her fruits."

existence, and making bread is the paradigmatic example of our partnership with God in His creation.

We add dates in the form of date honey (*silan*), mindful of the verse, "A righteous man will flourish like a date palm, like a cedar in the Lebanon he will grow tall. Planted in the House of the Lord, in the courtyards of our God they will flourish."[5] No part of the palm tree is wasted; it is a sustainable tree. The dates are eaten, the branches are used for waving on Sukkot,[6] the dried thatch is used for roofing, the fibers are used as ropes, the leaves can become sieves and the trunk can be used for house beams. From this we can learn that man should not to be wasteful in life, and that all parts of him should be used to carry out God's commandments.

Jews are compared to olive trees, therefore we pour olive oil, a product of the tree, into the challah to symbolize — much like Rosh Chodesh — our ability to renew ourselves. Olive trees have interesting characteristics: they can easily resist drought, diseases and even fire — the roots that remain regenerate the trees even when the ground is a smoky ruin — therefore they live many years. This might be one of the many reasons why Jews are compared to olive trees; we have the ability to regenerate ourselves through our faith, to start new and transcend all obstacles.

After the rising, we will knead figs into the dough , as a reminder that in the Talmud, fig trees are compared to Torah. Elucidating the verse in Proverbs, "He who tends a fig tree will eat its fruits,"[7] the Talmud explains that figs on a tree do not ripen all at once, and the more you search the tree, the more figs you find. Such is also the case with Torah — the more you meditate upon it, the more meanings come from it.[8]

Wine and grape juice are central to all Jewish celebrations because they are holy, sanctified beverages with a blessing all their own. We will add raisins to the dough to actualize the spiritual potential of grapes, imbuing our challah with holiness.

We will then shape our challah as a pomegranate, a fruit that had great significance in Ancient Israel, and signifies both fruitfulness and righteousness. It is said that there are 613 seeds in a pomegranate, corresponding to the 613 commandments found in the Torah. According to the Talmud, the 248 positive commandments correspond to the 248 limbs of the human body.[9] *Targum Yonatan*, written by a first-century sage who translated the prophetic books of the Bible, adds that the 365 negative commandments correspond to the 365 sinews in the human body.[10] Together, these add up to 613, alluding to the idea that you must use the physical body that God gave you to live as a Jew.

After the egg wash, we will adorn the challahs with barley grits, which is the first grain to ripen in the spring — a time when our taste buds can flourish after the barrenness of winter. We learn a lesson of faith and patience as we await its flowering, just as we do when we look at the dark sky of Rosh Chodesh, knowing that the moon will soon wax and grow.

---

5   Psalms 92:13-14

6   A closed branch from the palm tree, called the lulav, is one of the Four Species held and blessed on Sukkot. The other three are the hadass (myrtle), aravah (willow) and etrog (citron).

7   Proverbs 27:18

8   Babylonian Talmud, Tractate Eruvin 54a-b

9   Makkot 23B

10 Targum Yonatan Ben Uziel on Bereshit 1:27

Man is likened in the Torah to "a tree of the field." [11] The kabbalists understood this as a metaphor for how our lives mirror those of trees. A tree needs to be attached to its life source, the soil, in order to grow. In the human "tree," our roots are our faith. Our ability to affect others and to create new life constitutes our "fruits."

This meditation is about identifying with the fruits of the trees and reminding ourselves how we can affect others. We will endeavor to pass our knowledge and faith into the dough, allowing it to be shared by those who eat it. Kneading that kind of consciousness into the dough enhances the presence of God in our physical realm.

- Start with gentle belly breathing from the nose. This allows you to have more control over your breath. Slowly inhale and exhale, pulling your breath all the way into your belly. Feel your belly expand.

- Be totally present as you slowly inhale and exhale. If your mind wanders, calmly bring it back.

- Continue to focus on your breath and just your breath. Feel the difference in temperature between how the air goes in and how it goes out.

- Once you feel yourself enter a meditative state, imagine your body as the trunk of the tree, firmly planted on the ground, and your feet extended as roots into the ground. Your roots are your faith that binds you to God.

- Your arms are branches that sway in the wind, agile

11 Deuteronomy 20:19

and fruitful at the same time. Allow your awareness to extend into the challah, via your arms that work the dough.

- You are a fruit-bearing tree; this dough will form the fruits of your faith.

- Concentrate on the dough as an extension of you, becoming part of something greater. You are bonding with God in the process of transforming this dough into sustenance.

- After the meditation, smell a fragrant spice such as cloves to re-involve yourself with the physical world and make you feel grounded again.

Tasting and Blessing Godliness

Tu B'Shvat coincides with the renewal of budding in the trees. The early winter rains are mostly over, the sap in the trees has risen, and the period of budding is just beginning. This may be the reason that the rabbis of the *Mishna* designated this date as the "New Year" for trees, a date by which to calculate the tithing of fruit to the Levites, as commanded in Deuteronomy: "Every year, you shall set aside a tenth part of the yield…so that you may learn to revere your God forever" (14:22-23). While we can no longer tithe directly as our ancestors did, we can praise God through blessing and tasting as many fruits as possible on the day that is dedicated to them.

The kabbalists regarded eating from the seven species on Tu B'Shvat as a way of improving our spiritual selves, in line with the idea of *tikkun olam* — spiritually repairing the world. Rabbi Isaac Luria, the Arizal,[12] explained that there is a holiness inherent in nutrition: food is not simply organic molecules taken into your body to nourish it, but also contains divine sparks that move up to the brain and interact with our Godly soul.[13]

The very first sin man committed was one of improper eating; Adam and Eve's exile from the Garden of Eden came about when they ate the fruit from the Tree of Knowledge of Good and Evil. They mistakenly perceived this world as only a source of gluttonous bliss, rather than as a bridge to God. They grabbed pleasure, rather than recognizing that true ecstasy is not found in the taste of the fruits of the world, but in following the words of our Creator. The kabbalists taught that Tu B'Shvat is an opportune time for rectifying their transgression.

To contribute to the rectification of Adam and Eve's transgression, we contemplate and appreciate the seven species native to the Land of Israel, a wondrous loving gift from God. We praise Him for the taste, fragrance, beauty and nutrition they possess. The blessings are a thank-you note to our Creator, who created an endless variety of appetizing and nourishing foods for us to enjoy. God could easily have arranged for humans to be nourished by photosynthesis, like plants; instead He gave us taste buds, and many miraculous organs with which to eat and digest food. Eating of the fruit is a metaphor for our interaction with this world: correct consumption, with blessings and appropriate *kavanah*, leads to a perfected world and spiritual bliss, while incorrect consumption leads to destruction and spiritual degradation, as seen with Adam and Eve. The Talmud further elaborates that someone who eats and doesn't say a blessing is considered a thief, because every aspect of God's creation is inherently holy. A blessing re-infuses the world with holiness. Eating without a blessing, however, lowers the level of holiness in the world without replacing the loss and is regarded as theft.[14] God receives our gratitude when we bless our food, showing we are always conscious that He is the Ultimate Giver.

Interestingly, the *Mishna* calls Tu B'Shvat the New Year for the tree (*ilan*), rather than for trees (*ilanot*), plural.[15] According to the Zohar, the reason for this is to hint at a connection to the Tree of Knowledge in the Garden of Eden, which "puts forth blossoms bearing fruits of its kind." The Zohar explains that *'bearing fruit'* is a reference to the righteous person, who is the basis upon which the world rests, and *'of its kind'* means all human beings, who have in them the spirit of holiness, which is the blossom of that tree.[16] I like to think that there is an element of *tikkun* (rectification) that we can learn from this description of the tree. The *'bearing fruit'* is the woman who perpetuates the Jewish religion in words and in action, as with making challah. *'Of its kind'* is the woman who practices in her own way. Our challahs are individually made, and yet we are still furthering our Jewishness and bearing fruit for future generations.

---

12 The Arizal was a sixteenth-century kabbalist from Safed who revolutionized the study of contemporary Jewish mysticism.

13 Rabbi Isaiah Horowitz, known as The Shlah (1565-1630), quoted the Arizal in Kitzur Shnei Luchot, ha-brit Shaar Ha'Otiyot, ha Kedusha, p. 41. The Arizal used this verse to explain the principle: "Man does not live by bread alone, by the utterances of God's mouth does man live." (Deuteronomy 8:3) "Every piece of food has a body and a soul. The physically observable food is its body, the holy life force from Above that gives it its beings and qualities… its soul. When a soul eats it, then his soul derives enjoyment and sustenance from the soul of the food, and his body from the body of the food." This idea is originally found in the first section of Pri Etz Hadar, the text of the Tu B'Shvat seder. It was first published as a pamphlet in Venice in 1728.

14 Babylonian Talmud: Tractate Berachot 35b

15 Mishnah, Tractate Rosh Hashana, 1:1

16 Zohar Bereishit 33a on Genesis 1:11

Integrating the Seven Species into our challah is a way to make manifest our appreciation of and growth from the wisdom of the Torah. Whether you eat this challah on Shabbat, or on Tu B'Shvat itself, imagine that you are eating in the presence of God, in the Garden of Eden, celebrating the fruits of His trees that He has gracefully shared with us.

Reflective Questions

1. There were two trees in the center of the Garden of Eden: the Tree of Life (representing Torah and eternal life) and the Tree of Knowledge of Good and Evil (representing death). Why do you think Adam and Eve chose to eat from the Tree of Knowledge, especially since God commanded them not to?

2. The sages say that one is held accountable for not eating a new fruit when presented with the opportunity.[17] Why do you think this is so? What does this say about Judaism?

3. The Seven Species of produce that God blessed suggests a plant-based diet. Could you live on these seven ingredients, if not practically, then theoretically? What are your thoughts on the ancient diet of the Jews?

4. How are you mindful of the foods you consume? Do you appreciate the taste and texture? How it's sourced? Are there any special rituals you perform before or after eating?

5. In the Torah, man is compared to a "tree in the field." Can you relate to a tree? What is to be learned from the Seven Species (trees/plants) that God blessed for our own development?

6. Of all the seven species, which one do you most identify with, and why?

7. How do you show that you are grateful for the natural resources we have been blessed with?

Kavanah for Hafrashat Challah

Since the Holy Temple was destroyed, we can no longer bring the first fruits as offerings. On Tu B'Shvat we instead offer the fruit of our lips, to praise God for the Seven Species of the Land of Israel, and indeed, for all his bounty. Baking challah using produce indigenous to Israel is a way to make our gratitude manifest. Ask God to give you an opportunity to rectify Adam and Eve's sin of improper eating with this offering of *hafrashat challah*.

The procedure and blessing for the *hafrashat challah* ceremony can be found on pages 14-17. Participants may wish to shape the challah afterwards, or take it home and shape it there.

---

17 Jerusalem Talmud, Kiddushin 4:12

Boiled Egg in Challah *(Chubzeh di Purim)*

Traditionally, this challah hails from the Moroccan Jewish community, and is made for Purim. Two hard-boiled eggs are placed in the middle of the challah dough, to represent Haman's eyes as they bulge out of his head after he has been hanged.

Yields: 8 – 10 challahs

INGREDIENTS

4 tablespoons active dry yeast

4 ½ cups (1.1 liters) warm water

¾ cup (150 g) organic sugar plus 2 tablespoons organic sugar

5 pounds (2.25 kg) organic white flour

1 ½ tablespoons sea salt

1 cup (230 ml) neutral-tasting oil, such as safflower oil

10 hard-boiled eggs with shells

Topping

2 cage-free organic eggs, beaten

Sesame seeds, for topping

1 In a large bowl, combine the yeast with the 2 tablespoons of sugar and the warm water. Cover the bowl and allow the mixture to start activating. Yeast activation should take about 10 minutes; it will be bubbling and foamy.

2 Set 1 cup (125 g) of flour aside. Sift the remaining flour, sugar, and salt into the bowl.

3 Pour the yeast mixture and oil onto the flour. Combine all the ingredients, using a spatula. When it begins to form a dough, it is time to knead. At this point, you can remove the dough from the bowl and knead on the kitchen counter if it's easier for you, or directly in the bowl.

4 To knead the dough: grab the side of the dough furthest away from you and fold it toward yourself. Fold the dough in half and use your body weight to push the dough into itself. If you find that the dough is sticking too much to the surface and preventing you from kneading properly, dust the dough with flour. Give the dough a quarter turn (90 degrees). Grab the other side and fold it in half. Again, with a lot of weight behind it, push the newly folded half into itself. Repeat this process for 10-15 minutes, or until the dough is smooth, silky, elastic and the dough does not stick to the surface.

5 After the dough is thoroughly prepared, lay it on the countertop while you grease the bowl with a fine layer of oil. Next, turn the dough in the oil several times so that the dough is greased lightly on all sides.

6 Cover the bowl with a large plastic garbage bag or kitchen towel and allow it to rise for 1 hour.

7 Make the blessing on *hafrashat challah* — see **Hafrashat Challah, page 17.**

8 Knead the dough again for a few more minutes and then divide dough into 10 equal parts and roll out each part into a 10-inch (25 cm) circle, about ¼ inch (6 mm) thick. Use the remaining flour for the surface area and hands to prevent sticking.

9 Impress a hard-boiled egg into the center of each circle, enough to lodge it into the dough. Cut 2

separate slivers from the edge of the dough, about 3 inches (8 cm) long. The strips will be used to secure the eggs in place.

10 Lay the two strips in an X across the center top of the egg and secure tthe bottom of the strips to the dough.

11 Use the remaining strip to encircle the base of the egg.

12 Around the circumference of the dough, use scissors to cut fringes. Pinch together every other fringe, leaving a fringe in the middle untouched. Then pull the middle fringe on top of the pinched fringes and roll up. This will create a flower effect.

13 Don't let this challah rise as long as you normally would, as it would completely lose its shape. Limit the second rise to just 15 minutes. Pinch the ends again before glazing the challah with egg-wash.

14 If you cannot bake the challahs immediately, then this is the time to wrap the shaped dough in plastic wrap to prevent drying. You can store it in the coldest part of the refrigerator for up to 48 hours. On the day of baking, remove the dough from refrigerator and let stand on kitchen counter until it comes to room temperature, about one hour.

15 Preheat the oven to 350° F (180° C). If your dough has risen further and opened up the seams, pinch them closed. Prepare your egg wash and decorate the top of the challah with sesame seeds.

16 Bake in your preheated oven for about 25-30 minutes, or until loaves turn golden brown and shiny. Bread should have a nice hollow sound when thumped on the bottom.

17 Remove from the oven and cool on a rack. Wait at least one hour before serving. If you are freezing the challah, wrap in waxed paper and foil. It can be stored in the freezer for up to 2 months.

Before Preparing the Dough, recite optional Rosh Chodesh Psalms, page 19.

The Pregnant Year

In several places in the Torah we are instructed that we must celebrate Passover during spring: "Seven days you shall eat unleavened bread, as I commanded you, in the month of Aviv [Spring], for in the month of Aviv you came out of Egypt" (Exodus 34:18), and "Observe the month of Aviv, and keep the Passover to the Lord your God, for in the month of Aviv the Lord your God brought you out of Egypt by night" (Deuteronomy 16:1).

This commandment is potentially problematic; the dates of Jewish festivals may be determined by our lunar months, but seasons are dictated by the sun. As a lunar year is eleven days shorter than a solar year, if we always followed a calendar that consisted of twelve months, festivals would fall in different seasons, depending on the year. To avoid this problem, we keep our lunar calendar in synch with the solar year by adding an extra month, known as *Adar Alef*, every few years (seven out of nineteen). This Jewish leap year is known as *shana me'uberet*, a pregnant year. The major festival that falls during the month of Adar, Purim, is celebrated during *Adar Bet*, the second Adar, not the first.

A pregnant year is one in which the cycles of the moon and the sun become aligned through the creation of an extra month. Adar is known as a particularly joyful month in the Jewish calendar. The month of *Adar Alef* gives us thirty days more than usual for the joy of Adar to grow.

We will mark this idea by "impregnating" our challah with a hard-boiled egg, symbolic of the joy that gestates and develops through the month of *Adar Alef*. Much as a fetus grows, our joy increases through the thirty days of *Adar Alef* and the thirteen days of *Adar Bet* that lead us to Purim, where it reaches its pinnacle and is "born."

As we enter the month of Adar, we are commanded to be joyful, because historically it was a time of miracles for the people of Israel.[1] Joy enables an easier connection with the Divine. When we are joyous, we are whole and complete. This meditation is designed to elevate the *mitzvah* of making challah into a joyous act. As it says in Psalms, "Serve God with joy."[2]

- Start with gentle belly breathing from the nose. This allows you to have more control over your breath. Slowly inhale and exhale, pulling your breath all the way into your belly. Feel your belly expand.

- Be totally present as you slowly inhale and exhale. If your mind wanders, calmly bring it back.

- Continue to focus on your breath and just your breath. Feel the difference in temperature between how the air goes in and how it goes out.

- The challah is the vehicle through which you can joyfully reach toward God.

  Once you feel yourself enter a meditative state, direct your thoughts to the verse: "Serve God with joy."

- Concentrate on the meaning of the verse, allowing the spiritual power of your proclamation to filter through your mind and heart as it travels via your kneading hands to the dough.

- Breathe in joy. Let it fill you.

---

1 Babylonian Talmud, Ta'anit 29a

2 Psalms 100:2

- As you slowly exhale, express that joy through the kneading of the challah.

- Bask in the joyful energy of the month.

After the meditation is complete, smell a fragrant spice such as cloves to re-involve yourself with the physical world and help you feel grounded again.

Discussion during the Rising

Increasing Joy

Adar Alef gives us an extra thirty days of joyfulness before the advent of Purim — the most joyous time for the Jews because we prevailed over our Persian adversaries even when everything was stacked against us. When we enter *Adar Alef*, we have the opportunity and responsibility to infuse joy into our lives by thinking positive thoughts and focusing on the good.

Pregnancy is a time of anticipation and preparation for the joyful event of birth. When pregnant, a woman may take classes to prepare herself for the baby. Perhaps she will shop for baby furniture, think of colors for the nursery and discuss what the baby's name will be. The sight of a pregnant woman often evokes happiness. But you don't have to be pregnant to fill your life with joy. One of the ways to increase the joy in your life is by knowing that God wants you to be happy. Moshe Chaim Luzzatto, a rabbi and kabbalist who lived in Italy during the eighteenth century, explained that "…man was created for the sole purpose of rejoicing in God and deriving pleasure from the splendor of His presence. This is the greatest pleasure possible."[3] To achieve the

maximum amount of pleasure, God provided us with the Torah, and within it, the blueprint for existence. Torah study will provide us with methods to cleave to God through thought, speech and action, the three garments of the soul: "Thought, the faculty by which a person's soul expresses itself to the conscious self, is the innermost of the garments. Speech is the soul's vehicle of expression to others through words, whereas deed is the expression of the soul by way of tools of the material world."[4]

The first step is to manage our thoughts, and focus on the things that make us happy. This is where meditation comes in handy; practicing mindfulness everyday enables us to control erratic thoughts. The second step is to make a conscious effort to speak positively — about anyone and anything. We can start with the morning prayer upon awakening, *Modeh Ani*, which is a thank you to God for bringing us back to the waking world so that we may continue to do positive work here. We can look out of our windows and comment on what a beautiful day we are part of. Just by speaking kindly, we will automatically find ourselves participating in the third step — action — because we will be motivated to behave as though we are in a state of joy. "Jewish action" is doing divine work, and there are 248 positive commandments[5] that we can perform to express our joy for God. We can start by smiling, dancing, baking *challah* — one of those commandments is *hafrashat challah* — and getting together for a Rosh Chodesh group. All these positive behaviors affect the way we feel. The cumulative effect of increasing joy is to bring down our fences and extinguish harmful thoughts.

Man's Duty in the World

4   Rabbi Adin Steinsaltz, *Opening the Tanya: Discovering the Moral and Mystical Teachings of a Classic Work of Kabbalah*, (California, Jossey-Bass, 1st edition) p. 122

5   There are 248 positive commandments in the Torah. Seventy-seven of them are applicable and relevant today. See http://www.mussarleadership.org/mitzvot/77_mitzvot.html for a list.

---

3   Moshe Chaim Luzzatto, *The Path of the Just,* 1740, Chapter 1: Concerning

Adar Alef may be missing the celebrations of Purim, but it still has something important to contribute. This extra month keeps the two elements of the Jewish calendar, our lunar months and our solar cycle, in harmony. This harmony translates to joy, since Adar itself is the happiest of the Jewish months, and in a leap year, our Adar time is doubled. By coming first, *Adar Alef* opens the gate to the joy of Purim, which we will celebrate in full during *Adar Bet*. By gathering together in a Rosh Chodesh cohort, we do our part to illuminate the world with joyful actions.

Reflective Questions

1. What thoughts bring joy to you?

2. How do you think you can develop joy? Are there practices you could put in place to sustain that joy?

3. Why do you think that the term for leap year in Hebrew is a "pregnant year"?

4. How would you define the "garments of the soul?" How is your soul clothed?

5. How do your garments express your inner divinity?

Kavanah for Hafrashat Challah

The *mitzvah* of separating challah is recognized as a *segula*, a spiritual benefit, for an easy, safe birth. It is customary to separate challah at least once during the ninth month of pregnancy. As the extra month in the "pregnant year," *Adar Alef* represents the burgeoning, developing joy that will reach its apex and "birth" on Purim. Pray that God helps deliver us into spiritual joy.

The procedure and blessing for the *hafrashat challah* ceremony can be found on pages 14-17. Participants may wish to shape the challah afterwards, or take it home and shape it there.

Rose-shaped Challah with Raisins and Rosewater

Yields: 8 – 10 challahs

INGREDIENTS

4 tablespoons active dry yeast

4 ½ cups (1.1 liters) warm water

¾ cup (150 g) organic sugar plus 2 tablespoons organic sugar

5 pounds (2.25 kg) organic white flour

1 ½ tablespoons sea salt

1 cup (230 ml) olive oil

1 cup (150 g) raisins

Topping

2 cage-free organic eggs, beaten

1 teaspoon rosewater, in egg wash

Pistachio nuts, crushed with a mortar and pestle

Poppy seeds

Turbinado sugar

1 In a large bowl, combine the yeast with the 2 tablespoons of sugar and the warm water. Cover the bowl and allow the mixture to start activating. Yeast activation should take about 10 minutes; it will be bubbling and foamy.

2 Set 1 cup (125 g) of flour aside. Sift the remaining flour, sugar and salt into the bowl.

3 Pour the yeast mixture and oil onto the flour. Combine all the ingredients, using a spatula. When it begins to form a dough, it is time to knead. At this point, you can remove the dough from the bowl and knead on the kitchen counter if it's easier for you, or directly in the bowl.

4 To knead the dough: grab the side of the dough furthest away from you and fold it toward yourself. Fold the dough in half and use your body weight to push the dough into itself. If you find that the dough is sticking too much to the surface and preventing you from kneading properly, dust the dough with flour. Give the dough a quarter turn (90 degrees). Grab the other side and fold it in half. Again, with a lot of weight behind it, push the newly folded half into itself. Repeat this process for 10-15 minutes, or until the dough is smooth, silky, elastic and the dough does not stick to the surface.

5 After the dough is thoroughly prepared, lay it on the countertop while you grease the bowl with a fine layer of oil. Next, turn the dough in the oil several times so that the dough is greased lightly on all sides.

6 Cover the bowl with a large plastic garbage bag or kitchen towel and allow it to rise for 1 hour.

7 Make the blessing on *hafrashat challah* — see **Hafrashat Challah, page 17.**

8   Knead the raisins into the dough and then divide the dough into 8 equal parts. If the raisins pop out, just poke them back in. Use the remaining flour for the surface area and hands to prevent sticking.

9   Roll out each ball into a strand of about 2 feet (60 cm) long and 1 inch (about 2 cm) thick. Flatten the strand into a flat log, 2 inches (4 cm) wide.

10   Cut diagonal slits reaching halfway across the log at about 1 ½ inch (about 4 cm) intervals. Then coil the log around itself and pinch the end, forming a floral shape.

11   Cover the loaves again and let them rise in a warm place for 1 hour or until the dough has doubled in volume from its original size. The slits will look more petal-like at this point.

12   If you cannot bake the challahs immediately, then this is the time to wrap the shaped dough in plastic wrap to prevent drying. You can store it in the coldest part of the refrigerator for up to 48 hours. On the day of baking, remove the dough from refrigerator and let stand on kitchen counter until it comes to room temperature, about one hour.

13   Preheat the oven to 350° F (180° C). Prepare your egg wash with rose water and sprinkle with the pistachio nuts, poppy seeds, sesame seeds and turbinado sugar.

14   Bake in your preheated oven for about 30-35 minutes, or until loaves turn golden brown and shiny. Bread should have a nice hollow sound when thumped on the bottom.

15   Remove from the oven and cool on a rack. Wait at least one hour before serving. If you are freezing the challah, wrap in waxed paper and foil. It can be stored in the freezer for up to 2 months.

Before Preparing the Dough, recite optional Rosh Chodesh Psalms, page 19.

Introduction to Challah Theme during the Yeast Activation

A Time to Be Joyous

Purim, one of our most joyous holidays, commemorates a time when the Jewish people living in the ancient Persian Empire were saved from extermination. The sugar in this month's challah can represent the "sweet" turn of events — tragedy was averted, and transformed into triumph. The story of Purim is told in the biblical book of Esther (also known as *Megillat Esther*). It centers around a beautiful young Jewish woman, Esther, and her uncle, Mordechai, who raised her as his daughter. Esther and Mordechai lived in the capital city of the Persian Empire, Shushan.

The story opens when the king of Persia, Achashverosh, throws a lavish banquet that lasts for six months, culminating in a week-long feast for the residents of Shushan. At the party, he demands that his wife, Queen Vashti, dance naked for his pleasure in front of everyone. When she refuses to follow orders, she is beheaded. Achashverosh then orders that all young women in the capital be presented to him so that he may choose a new bride. Ultimately, Esther, hiding her Jewish identity, is chosen as his new queen.

According to the Talmud, Esther subsisted as a vegetarian in order to remain faithful to the laws of kashrut.[1] She had seven maids, one for each day of the week, and used their schedules to remind herself when Shabbat fell. With a different maid every day, they didn't see that she behaved differently on Shabbat, so she was able to maintain her secret. She did what she needed to do in

order to maintain her Jewish practices. To honor and commemorate Esther's vegetarian diet and her will to live as a Jew, we will be adorning our challahs with nuts and seeds after we shape them.

The villain of the story is Haman, an arrogant, egotistical advisor to the king. All the king's subjects are ordered to honor Haman and bow down to him. Everyone does, except Mordechai. Furious with Mordechai, and discovering that he is a Jew, Haman asks the king that he be allowed to exterminate the Jews in all 127 provinces of the empire. The king gives the fate of the Jewish people into Haman's hands. Haman draws lots (*purim*) to determine the date that this genocide will take place. The date is the thirteenth of the month of Adar.

The king signs a decree against the Jews, and when Mordechai hears it, he persuades Esther to speak to the king on behalf of the Jewish people. Esther tells Mordechai, "Go and gather together all the Jews and fast for me for three days."[2] After this fast, Esther approaches the king and invites him to a banquet, where she reveals her vulnerable Jewish identity, and pleads for her life and the lives of her people. She succeeds. Haman is hanged the next day, on gallows he had built for Mordechai. Although he cannot rescind his own decree, the king signs a second decree, stating that the Jews are allowed to preemptively kill those thought to be a risk. Haman's plan is foiled, and disaster is averted. Mordechai becomes a counselor to the king, and institutes an annual commemoration of the Jewish people's deliverance: the festival of Purim.

There is a poem recited on Purim, after the megilla has been read, which refers to the Jewish people as "the rose of Jacob." The first line of the poem reads: "The rose of Jacob thrilled with joy and exulted when they beheld Mordechai garbed in royal blue." The epicenter of the events of Purim was Shushan, a word similar

---

1   Targum Esther 2:7 and Midrash Panim Aherim 63 and 64. The Talmud, Megilla 13a, also mentions that Esther only ate permitted food, and one can therefore deduce that that would necessitate a vegetarian diet.

2   Esther 4:16

to *Shoshana* in Hebrew, which means rose. In honor of these 'roses,' the challah is shaped like a rose, and incorporates rosewater in the egg wash.

According to the *Midrash*, when Achashverosh threw the lavish banquet described at the beginning of the Book of Esther, he used the precious vessels that had been taken from the First Temple, in Jerusalem, before it was destroyed.[3] By doing so, he was denying God, asserting his belief that the prophecy that the Temple would be rebuilt was false. The Jews of Shushan attended the feast despite Mordechai's urging that they not go, and said nothing about this sacrilege. When they gathered at Esther's behest to fast, they were repenting this error, drawing out God's mercy in order to make their nation strong again. Ultimately, they retained their Jewish identities, and the Temple *was* rebuilt. To honor this, we are replacing the vegetable oil in our challah with olive oil. Olive oil can represent the strength and persistence of the Jewish people. The oil is only extracted from the olive through squeezing and compressing it, and then straining the oil to remove impurities. Much like the Jews, who, despite oppression, rise and prevail.

Although God's name is not mentioned once in the Book of Esther, the traditional understanding of the events of the book is that He was working behind the scenes to help us survive Haman's genocidal plan.[4] There is a reflection of this reality in the cycle of the moon, too. On Rosh Chodesh, the new moon is totally concealed and hidden. As we approach the 14th of Adar, and the festival of Purim, the moon waxes and its radiance grows. On the festival itself, it is gloriously full.

From a deeper perspective, we can see the fullness of the moon at Purim time as alluding to the salvation of the Jewish nation after a period of darkness. To represent the sweetness of God's hidden plan, raisins are hidden in the dough after the rising.

Meditation during Kneading

No outright miracles occurred in the Purim story. Rather, a series of natural events played out in such a way that a "hidden hand" directing the outcome of the story is made apparent. Our world seems to be running on its own, full of random, unrelated events, but in truth it is God, hiding behind the curtain, who is directing our experiences. To celebrate this concealment of the miraculous in the everyday, we *hide* ourselves by dressing up in costume, appearing as something else, our true selves hidden underneath the masquerade. One interesting connection we can make here is that, more often than not, we masquerade in order to conceal our deficiencies. Since Purim is a holiday of concealment and revelation, this meditation will focus on connecting us with our masked souls in order to bare our true selves.

- Start with gentle belly breathing from the nose. This allows you to have more control over your breath. Slowly inhale and exhale, pulling your breath all the way into your belly. Feel your belly expand.

- Be totally present as you slowly inhale and exhale. If your mind wanders, calmly bring it back.

- Continue to focus on your breath and just your breath. Feel the difference in temperature between how the air goes in and how it goes out.

- Once you enter a meditative state, use the knead — the pulling and stretching — to form your true self

---

3 Babylonian Talmud, Megillah 11a

4 Esther's role and valor is hinted at in the Torah verse where God says, "I will surely hide [My Face from them]" (Deuteronomy 31:18). In Hebrew, "I will surely hide," is haster astir, which is from the same root as the name Esther, and contains the same letters. The Sages commented that God hiding His Face may mean that God will conduct His guidance of the Jewish people in a non-obvious, hidden way (Babylonian Talmud, Tractate Hullin 139b).

within the dough. God formed Adam out of clay, just like a potter molds his vessels into different shapes. Imagine that you are potter to yourself. What do you look like? How do you want to look? These might be unanswerable questions, but the goal is to at least break through the mask.

- Concentrate on breaking through your mask, allowing the spiritual power of your knead to filter through your mind and heart as it travels from your hands to the dough.

- The dough yields to you as the boundary between the self and the mask dissolves. You are at one with the dough and God. This is your true self.

After the meditation is complete, smell a fragrant spice such as cloves to re-involve yourself with the physical world and help you feel grounded again.

Discussion during the Rising

Jewish Unity

In the Megillah we read about the edict of annihilation proclaimed against the Jews: "Then Haman said to the Achashverosh, 'There is a particular nation *scattered and dispersed* amongst the people in all your provinces. Their laws are different from those of every other people; moreover, they do not observe the king's laws. It does not befit the king to tolerate them. If it pleases the king, have a decree written for their destruction'.... The king responded to Haman, 'The money is given to you, and the people too, to do with as seems good to you'.... Letters [recording the edict] were sent by courier to all the royal provinces 'to destroy, to slay and to exterminate all Jews, from young to old, including small children

and women,' on a specific day, the thirteenth day of the twelfth month, which is the month of Adar, and to seize their goods as plunder." (Esther 3:8-13).

Haman knew that the Jews' weakness was that they were scattered. According to the Ibn Ezra,[5] when Haman described them as "scattered and dispersed," he was not just referring to their physical reality, that they lived in different places throughout the empire, but their spiritual reality, that they were not unified — not in commitment to each other, nor through faith in God. Although fifty thousand Jews had returned to Judea previously, and had begun to rebuild the Temple, most of the Jews chose to remain wherever they were, in exile. Moreover, the Jews of Persia, in particular, had assimilated somewhat into Persian culture. As mentioned earlier, they made no complaint when they saw Achashverosh use sacred vessels from the First Temple for his banquet. With the Jews in such a state, Haman believed that victory against them could be easily achieved.

When Mordechai heard of the decree, he urged Esther to approach the king, to try and use her influence to save the Jews. Esther was afraid to do this; anyone who came into the king's presence without first being summoned was subject to execution. Approaching him on her own initiative was very dangerous, no matter how favored she was. After all, Achashverosh had ordered the execution of his previous wife in a fit of anger. Esther's concern was very real.

To help summon Divine assistance, Esther called for all the Jews of Shushan to fast and pray for three days. In Judaism, fasting is seen as an expression of devotion and focus — saying that we are willing to ignore our physical needs in favor of our spiritual needs. Esther was about

---

5 Abraham ibn Ezra lived in Spain during the Middle Ages. He excelled in philosophy, mathematics, poetry, linguistics and exegesis; his commentaries on the Bible are usually included as standard in any edition of Tanach that includes exegesis.

to do something very chancy and very necessary; the fast was a means of asking the Jews to unite behind her through something more than ordinary prayer. That the Jews gathered together to fulfill her request restored the Jewish unity that had been lacking. There is *midrashic* commentary that claims that it was this redemptive unity that ultimately led to the nullification of Haman's decree. The Jews began an entirely new phase of service, which totally transcended that of the previous months.

There is a powerful, resonant tradition that links the story of Purim, one in which the name of God is not overtly mentioned, with *Matan Torah*, the giving of the Torah on Mount Sinai, when God was not only explicitly present, but heard by the entire Jewish people. According to the Talmud, the Jews were not really given a true choice to accept the Torah when it was offered to them at Mount Sinai. God suspended the mountain over the Jews and coerced them into accepting it, warning them: "If you accept the Torah, it is well, and if not, here shall be your grave." So when the Israelites said "*na'aseh v'nishma*," "we will do and we will listen," it wasn't a genuine, full acceptance, but one given under duress. The Talmud compares this to the situation of the Jews in the Book of Esther. At the end of the book, when we read that the customs of Purim are being established to be celebrated on a holy day, as a celebration and recognition of God's role in the redemption of the Jews from destruction, it says that: "The Jews established and accepted" (Esther 9:27). This is the only occasion in Tanach,[6] other than when they were standing at Sinai, when the Jews officially proclaim that they accept laws upon themselves. The rabbis of the Talmud saw this connection as evidence that only in Persia, a thousand years after Sinai, did the Jews accept voluntarily what they had been coerced into accepting previously. Moreover, they did so when God's actions were hidden behind those of man. According to this tradition, Shavuot may be the festival when we celebrate the *giving* of the Torah, but Purim is the festival when we celebrate its *acceptance.*[7]

It was at a final banquet described in the *megillah* that Esther and Mordechai decreed that Purim should be celebrated: "And these days should be celebrated by every generation, and by every family, and by every province, and by every city, and these days of Purim should never cease amongst the Jews" (Esther 9:28) and "… observe them as days of feasting and joy, for sending gifts to one another and gifts to the poor" (Esther 9:22). In this way, we foster solidarity amongst ourselves forever. On the day of Purim, we send our friends *Mishloach Manot*, literally "sending of portions," ready-to-eat foods that can be eaten during the special festival Purim banquet. This challah that we make today can be sent as *Mishloach Manot*. The reason for this *mitzvah* is twofold; to ensure that everyone has sufficient food for the Purim banquet, and to increase love and friendship between Jews. It provides an ideal opportunity to embrace our fellow Jews, irrespective of any religious or social differences.

Let us honor and commemorate the solidarity that the Jews of Shushan demonstrated with our gathering today on Rosh Chodesh. We are women from all walks of life who give a part of ourselves to the making of this challah, which we will then share with others, further fostering Jewish unity. *Am Yisrael Chai*!

Reflective Questions

1. Can you think of a potential modern day Purim story — a looming annihilation of the Jews that has occurred? Or is presently occurring? Do you think there are actions you could take upon yourself to avert a disaster? What do you think of that notion?

---

6 Tanach is an acronym for "Torah" — the Five Books of Moses, "Nevi'im" — the Books of the Prophets, and "Ketuvim" or Writings, the final part of the Jewish Bible.

7 Talmud Shabbat 88a

2. Do you think you would have said something at Achashverosh's banquet about the Temple's vessels being used, bearing in mind that you would have been a guest?

3. In the Book of Esther, Haman describes the Jews as "scattered and dispersed." Do you think that "Jewish unity" is the ultimate way to draw God down to earth?

4. Imagine yourself in Persia. Upon hearing of a genocide being planned against the Jews, would you have any hope that you would be able to defeat the Persian army? In fact, the Jews did. Can you fathom how?

5. In the entire Book of Esther, God's name is not mentioned at all. Why do you think this is so?

6. Why is it important to have a book in the Torah that acknowledges hidden miracles?

7. Can you think of a hidden miracle in your life?

Kavanah for Hafrashat Challah

The *kavanah* before separating the challah is about honoring God by supporting His workers. We are all God's workers. On the day of Purim, it is a special *mitzvah* to give two different ready-to-eat food items to foster Jewish unity by supporting one another, in the form of *mishloach manot.* Ask God to help make our nation strong by helping us to remain united no matter our differences.

The procedure and blessing for the *hafrashat challah* ceremony can be found on pages 14-17. Participants may wish to shape the challah afterwards, or take it home and shape it there.

IN PREPARATION: In the invitation to this month's gathering, ask the participants to bring leftover wheat flour from their pantry. In this way, everyone comes together to rid their homes of *chametz* before Passover. Be sure to ask how much flour tthey are bringing so, if need be, the host can add more or less flour. In the event that you have a lot of flour to bake with, perhaps consider selling the extra pitas and use the proceeds for a Jewish cause.

Pita

Yields: 30 6-inch (15 cm) pitas

INGREDIENTS

4 tablespoons active dry yeast

4 cups (1liter) warm water

2 tablespoons organic sugar

5 pounds (2.25 kg) organic white flour

2 tablespoons sea salt

⅔ cup (150 ml) neutral tasting oil, such as safflower oil

1. In a large bowl, combine the yeast with the 2 tablespoons of sugar and the warm water. Cover the bowl and allow the mixture to start activating. Yeast activation should take about 10 minutes; it will be bubbling and foamy.

2. Set 1 cup (125 g) of flour aside. Sift the remaining flour and salt into the bowl. With a spatula, combine the ingredients. Once the ingredients come together as dough, it is time to knead. At this point, you can remove the dough from the bowl and knead on the kitchen counter if it's easier for you, or directly in the bowl.

3. To knead the dough: grab the side of the dough furthest away from you and fold it toward yourself. Fold the dough in half and use your body weight to push the dough into itself. If you find that the dough is sticking too much to the surface and preventing you from kneading properly, dust some flour on the dough. Give the dough a quarter turn (90 degrees). Grab the other side and fold it in half. Again, with a lot of weight behind it, push the newly folded half into itself. Repeat this process for 10-15 minutes or until the dough is smooth, silky, elastic and does not stick to the surface.

4. After the dough is thoroughly prepared, grease the large bowl with a fine layer of oil, turning the dough in the oil several times so that the dough is greased lightly on all sides.

5   Cover the bowl with a large plastic garbage bag or kitchen towel and allow it to rise for 40 minutes.

6   Make the blessing on *hafrashat challah* — see **Hafrashat Challah, page 17.**

7   Knead the dough again for a few more minutes and then divide the dough into 30 balls. Use the remaining flour for the surface area and hands to prevent sticking. Roll each piece into a 6-inch (15 centimeters) pancake. Cover with kitchen towel and let them rise again in a warm place for 20 minutes.

8   Place approximately six pitas on the hot cookie sheet, separating each pita by 2 inches (5 centimeters). Bake on the bottom rack for 3-4 minutes, flip over and then bake for another 2 minutes. You want the pitas puffed and lightly colored, not browned. Continue this process in batches until all pitas are baked.

9   If the pita puffs up once out of the oven, gently pierce it with a fork. Wrap the pitas in a towel till they are cool, then store in plastic bags until ready for use. You can store in the freezer for up to 2 months to retain freshness.

Before Preparing the Dough, recite optional Rosh Chodesh Psalms, page 19.

Breaking the Chain

Passover begins on the night of the 14th of Nissan and lasts seven or eight days, depending on whether you live in Israel or the Diaspora.[1] The Passover Seder teaches that every generation is required to tell the story of the Exodus, and that participants in this telling are to see themselves as though they, too, were slaves leaving Egypt.[2] We are required to relate to the story as supremely relevant to our lives today. Passover celebrates the birth of the Jewish nation.

The bread of our ancestors had no time to rise because they were expelled from Egypt: "And they baked unleavened cakes of the dough which they brought out of Egypt, for it was not leavened; because they were driven out of Egypt and could not delay, neither had they prepared for themselves any provision" (Exodus 12:39). We are commanded to eat *matzah*, unleavened flat bread, in commemoration of this historical circumstance. Moreover, we are commanded to search out and rid our homes of *all* leaven (*chametz*), before Passover begins.

In the ancient world, bread was usually made by using a type of sourdough starter. A little bit of raw dough was set aside, unbaked, in a cool, shaded place; this dough was then used as the leavening agent for the next week's bake. Preparing leavened bread required the use of old matter; a bacterial culture that was continuously fermenting in an unbroken chain of bread baking with

no beginning and no end. Perhaps this is why God demands that our cleansing each spring be total; we need to break all the chains that fetter us to the past. We must clear out all of the old from the house to make way for the new.

The ancient Hebrew word for leaven, or yeast, is *se'or*. There are no coincidences in the Hebrew language, and often there are multiple meanings within one word. The root of the word *lehash'ir*, which means to leave behind, is *se'or*. We can see this as an allusion to the Passover theme of leaving the past behind to start a new beginning. The "chain" of sourdough starter that was used constantly can be seen as a metaphor for the chains of slavery. The plainness and simplicity of matzah can be reinterpreted as a clean slate, the new beginning of the freed slave.

You have all been asked to bring your leftover flour in preparation for cleaning out last year's chains to the past. We are making pita, a type of round flatbread. Although pita is leavened, as a flatbread it is similar to the Yemenite and Iraqi matzah, which is soft, rather than crisp like most matzah. The circular shape can serve as an illustration of renewal, as we move through the cycle of the year to re-enter the spring season once more, and with it, the beginning of the Jewish year.[3]

This meditation will focus on our desire for a personal redemption from any aspect of ourselves which holds us back from achieving our full potential. We will be using our breath to clear out "*chametz*" — chains that keep us bonded to the past.

---

1 Days in the Jewish calendar begin at sundown, so Passover truly begins on the 15th of Nissan, but in practical terms, it is the night of the 14th day of the month.

2 Talmud, Pesachim 116b

3 The first of Nissan is the beginning of one of the four New Years in the Jewish calendar: it is the New Year for kings, and for the festive calendar.

- Start with gentle belly breathing from the nose. This allows you to have more control over your breath. Slowly inhale and exhale, pulling your breath all the way into your belly. Feel your belly expand.

- Be totally present as you slowly inhale and exhale. If your mind wanders, calmly bring it back.

- Continue to focus on your breath and just your breath. Feel the difference in temperature between how the air goes in and how it goes out.

- Once you feel yourself enter a meditative state, focus on any one thought, fear or action that you know keeps you in a restricted state. Do not overthink this, just focus on whatever comes to you in this moment.

- Continue belly breathing, counting to four while you breathe in. Allow the inhaled breath to travel to the hidden corners of your soul.

- On your out breath, exhale from your mouth until the count of five, expelling the *chametz* that is within you.

- Continue to breathe this way, mindful of each breath's purpose — to clear the *chametz* from your life.

- Use the knead to focus your intention.

After the meditation is complete, smell a fragrant spice such as cloves to re-involve yourself with the physical world and help you feel grounded again.

Out with the Old, In with the New

The Passover story begins over three thousand years ago. The twelve sons of Jacob and their families had immigrated to Egypt during a time of famine. Joseph was viceroy of Egypt, but after his death, a new Pharaoh came to power. This Pharoah dismissed Joseph's illustrious past and became worried about the growing numbers of Israelites, essentially foreigners, living in his land. Eventually, to limit their growth, he enslaved them, ultimately going so far as to order the murder of all male babies. One family tried to save their little one; his mother and older sister left their home and hid the baby in a basket, which they placed in the reeds that grew on the bank of the Nile. Pharaoh's daughter, identified in the *midrash* as Batya, found the baby and decided to raise him as her son, naming him Moses.

After Moses had reached adulthood, he ventured out of the palace and saw an Egyptian taskmaster whipping an Israelite, witnessing firsthand the brutality of the Egyptians. Angered, he killed the taskmaster and formed an allegiance in his heart with the Israelites. Subsequently, Moses had to flee Egypt; when it became known that he had killed an Egyptian, his own life was at stake. He fled to the neighboring region of Midian, where he married, had children, and lived for many years as a shepherd. When Moses grew old his world was turned upside down. Taking out his flocks as usual to the desert, he encountered God in the form of a "burning bush."

God sent Moses back to Egypt to demand the release of the Israelites from Pharaoh. At first, Moses refused to go; but ultimately he had no choice, and he reluctantly complied. God sent his older brother, Aaron, to help him. When Moses and Aaron confronted Pharaoh, and told him to let the Israelites go, he scornfully denied all knowledge of Moses' God and refused their demand. Moses then told Pharaoh that God would bring plagues against the Egyptian people if he did not cooperate. Pharaoh's heart was hardened and so the plagues began, becoming more and more severe. Pharaoh was given many chances to change his mind, but he continued to insist on keeping the Israelites as slaves.

On the first of Nissan, after the ninth plague (darkness), God told Moses that on the fourteenth day of the month every family should gather in their homes and eat meat from a slaughtered lamb — the paschal lamb. Then they were to mark their doorposts and lintels with the blood of the lamb, and not to exit their houses for the remainder of that night. The final plague that fell upon Egypt was "the death of the firstborn." The blood that marked the doors of the Israelite homes was a sign to God to "pass over" the homes and leave the inhabitants unscathed. Everywhere else in Egypt, any firstborn son or animal died. Pharaoh was devastated when his eldest son died, and he finally relented. He called for Moses and ordered him to leave with his people immediately, which they did.

Three days later, Pharaoh reneged on his decision. He led his army in a chase after the Israelites, who at that moment were cut off from any avenue of escape by the Red Sea. As the Egyptians neared, God miraculously parted the sea. The Israelites walked on dry land, with two huge walls of water on either side. When the Egyptian army tried to follow, the walls of water closed in on them. The Hebrew name for Egypt is *Mitzrayim*, which is connected to the word *metzar*, meaning either "distress" or "a narrow place." The Israelites escaped from Egypt, a distressing, narrow place, through the parted waters of the Red Sea. When the moon reached its fullness on the 15th of Nissan, a new reality was born for the Jewish nation — the reality of freedom.

Prior to the Exodus from Egypt, God gave the Israelites

their very first commandment as a people: to mark and sanctify the months of the year: "The renewal of the moon shall be unto you the festival of the head of the month, it shall be unto you the first of the months of the year (Exodus 12:2)."[4] You might wonder: what is freedom, if you are immediately given a new set of laws to follow? The laws of God are radically different from the laws of man. The Israelites were given their physical freedom by God in order to imbue divinity into their lives. The Israelites became free not in the sense of living without boundaries, but rather in order to devote themselves spiritually through a physical existence.

Why did God preface the Exodus not just with a commandment, but with the specific commandment of observing the New Moon? On the simplest level, it is a vital *mitzvah* — it gives us the correct framework within which to keep the rest of the commandments. There are, however, further levels of meaning in connecting the Israelite Exodus from Egypt with the sanctification of the moon. First, it can be proposed that the *mitzvah* of sanctifying the new moon was given to our ancestors in Egypt, a place of spiritual darkness, to illustrate the idea that the new moon has the ability to bring light even within a dark reality. Moreover, the moon produces no light of its own; its light is only a reflection of the light of the sun. This characteristic is why, in rabbinic literature, the Jewish people are often compared to the moon. Just as the moon reflects the light of the sun, the mission of the Jewish people — a mission given to them at Sinai — is to reflect the "light" of God, through His Torah, to the rest of the world.

When it seemed that all hope was gone for the Israelites, who had lived for generations in bondage; when it seemed as though they would be engulfed entirely by the darkness of oppression, defilement and persecution,

---

4   Nissan became the first month of the Hebrew calendar, though years were counted from the first of Tishrei, the seventh month.

they, like the moon, were renewed. This renewal could only take place when the Israelites let go of their past — the past that like the *se'or* was an unending chain of old matter. To make room for a spiritual life, they had to banish their abusive past completely. Fittingly, in the Torah, the month of Nissan is known as *Aviv*, spring. The Israelites were renewed as a nation during the month when nature is also renewing itself.

Reflective Questions

1. When you eat matzah on Passover does it mean something significant to you on a symbolic level? Do you eat it as a custom, or do you find deeper meaning in it? Do you find it relevant to our modern existence?

2. Is cleaning out chametz something important to you or is it just something you relate to on a traditional level?

3. Do we really need to clean out our house before Passover by turning everything upside down and inside out?

4. The author suggests that leavened bread is like a chain from the past that you need to break in order to be renewed. Do you agree with this definition? Can you break away from something while still holding on to it?

5. What characteristics of the moon do you identify with?

6. How can we use the story of Passover to find freedom in our own lives?

7. How do you define freedom?

Kavanah for Hafrashat Challah

This month, we will add a layer of significance to the *mitzvah* of separating challah. Not only is it a commemoration of our support of the priests in their Godly service, but we will also look on it as a commemoration of when our ancestors kept back a small portion of their dough to act as a starter for their next batch of bread. Usually we burn the separated dough because we can no longer give it to the priests, and are forbidden to eat it. This month we will see it, too, as symbolic of cutting our chains to the past. May we be blessed with true renewal this year: in our souls, in our homes and the world over. May our personal redemption lead to the full and final collective redemption of our people.

The procedure and blessing for the *hafrashat challah* ceremony can be found on pages 14-17. Participants may wish to shape the challah afterwards, or take it home and shape it there.

Pull-Apart Challah (*Yud-Bet* [12] Challah) with Silan and Olive Oil

Yields: 8 medium challahs

INGREDIENTS

4 tablespoons active dry yeast

4 ½ cups (1.1 liters) warm water

2 tablespoons organic sugar

1 (12-ounce) container of date honey (silan)

5 pounds (2.25 kg) organic white flour

1 ½ tablespoons sea salt

1 cup (230 ml) olive oil

Topping

2 cage-free organic eggs, beaten

Barley flakes

Sesame seeds (optional)

Poppy seeds (optional)

1. In a large bowl, combine the yeast with the 2 tablespoons of sugar and the warm water. Cover the bowl and allow the mixture to start activating. Yeast activation should take about 10 minutes; it will be bubbling and foamy.

2. Set 1 cup (125 g) of flour aside. Sift the remaining flour, silan honey and salt into the bowl.

3. Pour the yeast mixture and oil onto the flour. Combine all the ingredients, using a spatula. When it begins to form a dough, it is time to knead. At this point, you can remove the dough from the bowl and knead on the kitchen counter if it's easier for you, or directly in the bowl.

4. To knead the dough: grab the side of the dough furthest away from you and fold it toward yourself. Fold the dough in half and use your body weight to push the dough into itself. If you find that the dough is sticking too much to the surface and preventing you from kneading properly, dust the dough with flour. Give the dough a quarter turn (90 degrees). Grab the other side and fold it in half. Again, with a lot of weight behind it, push the newly folded half into itself. Repeat this process for 10-15 minutes, or until the dough is smooth, silky, elastic and the dough does not stick to the surface.

5. After the dough is thoroughly prepared, lay it on the countertop while you grease the bowl with a fine layer of oil. Next, turn the dough in the oil several times so that the dough is greased lightly on all sides.

6. Cover the bowl with a large plastic garbage bag or kitchen towel and allow it to rise for 1 hour.

7. Make the blessing on *hafrashat challah* — see **Hafrashat Challah, page 17.**

8. Knead the dough again for a few more minutes. Use the remaining flour for the surface area and hands to prevent sticking.

9   Divide the dough into 8 equal parts and then further divide each part into 12 separate balls by rolling each one in the palms of your hands to the size of a golf ball.

10 Place a larger ball in the center of the foil cake pan and the remaining balls around the center. The balls do not need to touch, as they will grow together as they rise.

11 Cover the loaves again and let them rise in a warm place for 1 hour or until the dough has doubled in volume from its original size. If you cannot bake the challahs immediately, then this is the time to wrap the shaped dough in plastic wrap to prevent drying. You can store it in the coldest part of the refrigerator for up to 48 hours. On the day of baking, remove the dough from the refrigerator and let stand on the kitchen counter until it comes to room temperature, about one hour.

12 Preheat the oven to 350° F (180° C). Prepare your egg wash and decorate the top of the challah with barley flakes or other optional toppings.

13 Bake in your preheated oven for about 30-35 minutes, or until loaves turn golden brown and shiny. Bread should have a nice hollow sound when thumped on the bottom.

14 Remove from the oven and cool on a rack. Wait at least one hour before serving. If you are freezing the challah, wrap in waxed paper and foil. It can be stored in the freezer for up to 2 months.

Before Preparing the Dough, recite optional Rosh Chodesh Psalms, page 19.

Manna from Heaven

This month we are going to represent the twelve tribes of Israel who left Egypt with a *Yud-Bet* Challah — a challah made up of twelve connecting balls.[1] A month after the Israelites left Egypt, on the fifteenth of Iyar, they reached the Wilderness of *Sin*.[2] Having consumed all the food they had brought with them from Egypt, they began to complain that they had been brought out of slavery merely to die of starvation in the desert. God answered that he would rain down bread from heaven: "Then said the Lord to Moses, Behold, I will rain bread from heaven for you; and the people shall go out and gather a certain portion every day…" (Exodus 16:4). This heavenly bread that was to sustain the Israelites during their time in the desert made its first appearance in Iyar. The Israelites named this heavenly bread manna, or *man*: "And when the children of Israel saw it, they said one to another, *Man-hu* (what is it?): for they knew not what it was" (16:15).

The manna was white, and looked similar to coriander seed. In the Torah it is described as tasting like wafers made with honey (Exodus 16:31), and like oil cake (Numbers 11:8). To commemorate the taste of manna, we will be using olive oil and date honey *(silan)* in our challah this month.

Our sages note that Iyar is an acronym for *"Ani Hashem Rofecha,"*[3] which means, "I am God your Healer." From a kabbalistic perspective, the primary causes for illness are either the eating of improper foods, or improper digestion and assimilation.[4] As the month when the Israelites began eating manna, which contained no waste and was totally assimilated into the body,[5] Iyar became associated with the heavenly food's healing influence.[6] Perhaps God created the manna with medicinal properties to help heal the Israelites of their years of emotional and physical deprivation as slaves — God nursing them, in much the same way as a mother nurses her infant. This would explain the *midrash* which states that the manna had miraculous properties: to children it tasted like mothers' milk; to youths, like bread; to the old, like honey; and to the sick, like barley soaked in oil and honey.[7] The manna was nurturing the Israelites through their "infancy," helping them form into a true nation so as to be ready to receive the Torah the following month, on Shavuot.

Many of the customs surrounding how we present challah at our Shabbat table today have evolved around stories of the manna. Each morning it rained down upon the desert floor, but to protect it, dew formed around it. This is one of the reasons that we place our challah on a decorative board, and cover it with a decorative cover — to commemorate the dew that encapsulated the manna. After we shape the challah, we may sprinkle it with sesame or poppy seeds to recall the manna that glittered like jewels in the early morning sun. Enough fell each day to feed every Israelite and, no matter how much people collected, it always worked out to one *omer* (a measure of about two quarts) per person. Anything

---

1 Yud-Bet equals twelve, according to the numerical value of the Hebrew alphabet.

2 This is a geographic area mentioned in the Torah as lying between Elim and Mount Sinai. Sin does not refer to sinfulness, but is an untranslatable word that would best translate as the moon. Biblical scholars suspect that the name Sin refers to the semitic moon-deity Sin, who was worshipped widely around the entire periphery of pre-Islamic Arabia, the Levant and Mesopotamia. (Adam Stone, 'Nanna/Suen/Sin (god),' *Ancient Mesopotamian Gods and Goddesses,* Oracc and the UK Higher Education Academy, 2013 [http://oracc.museum.upenn.edu/amgg/listofdeities/nannasuen/] Accessed 4/29/14)

---

3 Exodus 15:26

4 B'nei Yissaschar, by Rabbi Tzvi Elimelech of Dinov. Volume II, First Discourse on Iyar.

5 Talmud Yoma 75b

6 B'nei Yissaschar, Ibid.

7 Exodus Rabbah 5:9

that was left overnight rotted. Because manna did not fall on Shabbat, as it was a holy day, the Israelites were commanded to collect a double portion on Friday. This extra did *not* rot, and was eaten on Shabbat.[8] We use two loaves of challah for every Shabbat and festive meal to commemorate and represent this double portion of manna.

There is another *omer* with a connection to the month of Iyar. During Temple times, on the second day of Passover, an *omer* of the first cutting of the barley harvest was brought to the Temple as an offering. From that day we were instructed to count seven weeks, which would bring us to Shavuot.[9] These weeks are still counted today, and are known as *Sefirat Ha'Omer*, the Counting of the Omer, even though the *omer* offering is no longer brought. Although the counting begins in Nissan and ends in Sivan, we count through the entire month of Iyar, where *most* of the counting takes place. We will be using barley flakes as a topping for our challah to recall the ancient barley offering.

Meditation during Kneading

The month of Iyar is the midpoint between our ancestors' exodus from Egypt, in Nissan, and their receiving of the Torah the following month, in Sivan. Since it is a transitional month, Iyar can be seen as a month of building ourselves, from the foundation up, to become worthy to receive the Torah on Shavuot. In Hebrew, meditation is called *hitbonenut,* which comes from the root word *bo-neh,* meaning build. According to the Kabbalah, we can use these 49 days to build spiritual maturity through a focus on seven attributes, or *sefirot,*[10] each of which corresponds to one of the weeks of the Omer. *Sefirot*, in Kabbalah, are attributes or qualities through which God reveals Himself and continuously creates the world. The seven attributes (out of a total of ten) are **Chesed,** loving-kindness, benevolence; **Gevurah**, justice, discipline, restraint; **Tiferet**, beauty, harmony, compassion; **Netzach**, endurance, ambition; **Hod**, humility; **Yesod**, bonding, foundation; and **Malchut**, nobility, leadership.[11]

The first week of Iyar is the third week of counting the Omer; therefore the attribute to focus on is *Tiferet,* beauty. The quality of *Tiferet* is defined as blending the attributes of *Chesed*, loving-kindness, and *Gevurah*, discipline:

> *"Tiferet — compassion — blends and harmonizes the free outpouring love of chesed with the discipline of gevurah. Tiferet possesses this power by introducing a third dimension — the dimension of truth, which is neither love nor discipline and therefore can integrate the two. Truth is accessed through selflessness: rising above your ego and your predispositions enables you to realize truth. A clear and objective picture of yours and others needs. The imbalance of love and discipline (and for that matter, any distortion) is a result of a subjective, hence limited perspective; introducing truth, by suspending personal prejudices, allows you to express your feelings (including the synthesis of chesed and gevurah) in the healthiest manner. This quality gives tiferet its name, which means beauty: it blends the differing colors of love and discipline, and this harmony makes it beautiful."[12]*

---

8 Exodus 16:17-30

9 "You shall count for yourselves seven weeks, from when the sickle is first put to the standing crop shall you begin counting seven weeks. Then you will observe the Festival of Shavuot for the Lord your God" (Deuteronomy 16:9-10).

10 *Sefirot,* a kabbalistic term, should not be confused with *Sefirat [Ha'Omer],* even though the words are very similar.

11 See http://www.inner.org/sefirot/sefirot.htm

12 Simon Jacobson, A Spiritual Guide to the Counting of the Omer (Meaningful Life Center: NY 1996), Week Three.

According to Kabbalah, each of the ten *sefirot* can be associated with a particular part of the human body. *Chesed*, loving-kindness, is located in the right arm, which operates to draw others near; *Gevurah*, discipline, in the left, restrains. *Tiferet*, beauty and compassion, is in the middle — the center point of the body, which mediates between *Chesed* and *Gevurah*.

The purpose of this meditation is to help you experience these three energies harmonizing, embodied within you, through the kneading process. You will unite them. Before you begin the meditation, think of a situation that troubles you, an issue in your own life that you need to work through, or a person with whom you have a relationship that needs improving.

- Begin with gentle belly breathing from the nose. This allows you to have more control   over your breath. Slowly inhale and exhale, pulling your breath all the way into your belly. Feel your belly expand.

- Be totally present as you slowly inhale and exhale. If your mind wanders, calmly bring it back.

- Continue to focus on your breath and just your breath. Feel the difference in temperature between how the air goes in and how it goes out.

- Once you feel yourself enter a meditative state, draw your focus to *Gevurah,* discipline and judgment. Direct your attention to the issue you have chosen to focus on. Think about the ways you may be judging yourself or the other.

- Focus your attention on your left arm, which will express your thoughts, and the emotions they bring up. Perhaps you want to clench a fist or push something away. Maybe your muscles tighten. Use the kneading process to express that feeling.

- Next, try to think of the same issue or person not with judgment, but with love, sympathy and kindness. Try to fully explore this perspective, experiencing the feelings of *Chesed* in a boundless way.

- Draw your attention to your right arm, which will express what you are feeling via the kneading of the dough. Use your arm to bring this loving-kindness towards you. Don't worry if it seems strange. Just give it a try, with an open, curious mind, and the open heart that is necessary for experiencing loving-kindness.

- Don't overthink it; just feel these two energies, *Chesed* on the right side and *Gevurah* on the left.

- We are going to bring these two polarized emotions together. We will harmonize *Chesed* and *Gevurah*.

- Focus on both arms moving together at the same tempo and sway your whole body to move with your arms. Mediate between them — dance with them. This is *Tiferet*.

- You are now using the might of discipline in your left arm to moderate and channel your innate desire for loving-kindness. You can cultivate this consciousness and express it in the body via the kneading. Stand still in this place of integration, being centered on *Tiferet* in the heart center. You are experiencing truth.

After the meditation is complete, smell a fragrant spice such as cloves to re-involve yourself with the physical world, and help you feel grounded again.

A New Nation in Development

During the month of Nissan, we became a nation. We were borne out by God from Egypt, a narrow, constrained place, to the transformative open space of the desert. In Iyar, the Jewish people entered adolescence; we struggled to become a mature nation, worthy of receiving the Torah. Inherently, therefore, Iyar is connected to the idea of spiritual growth. This facet of Iyar can even be seen when looking at the agricultural cycle of the land of Israel.

The holidays of Pesach and Shavuot had agricultural significance as well as historical and religious significance. Pesach marked the beginning of the barley harvest, while Shavuot marked the beginning of the wheat harvest. In ancient times, barley was viewed as inferior to wheat; the diet of animals and the poor. That the barley harvest falls on the second day of Passover and the wheat harvest begins at Shavuot creates a compelling metaphor for our spiritual task during *Sefirat Ha'Omer*: there is a transition we ourselves must make, from the inferior to the superior grain. During those forty-nine days of counting, our task is to work on refining ourselves, striving to transform and elevate our base emotions and impulses. We need to leave Egypt, the place of our bondage, not just physically but spiritually.

The essential *mitzvah* of counting *Sefirat Ha'Omer* is achieved, literally, through counting. Every night during the evening service, the day and the week of the Omer is recited, together with a blessing. The kabbalistic interpretation of *Sefirat Ha'Omer* is one of striving for spiritual growth through the seven *sefirot* (attributes), one per week of the *Omer*. Each of these seven *sefirot* in turn subdivides into seven, making a total of forty-nine, one per day of the *Omer*. So, for example, the first week of *sefirah* is dedicated to *Chesed* — the attribute of loving-kindness. On Day One of Week One we deal with *Chesed in Chesed*

— the aspect of loving-kindness in loving-kindness. On Day Two, we focus on *Gevurah* in *Chesed* — the aspect of strength, or discipline, in loving-kindness. And so on. Each day has a unique energy flow to be tapped and channeled.

The Kabbalah teaches that there is benefit in focusing on the specific aspect of each attribute on the particular day of the *Omer* on which it falls. To live productive and liberated lives we need to cultivate a state of harmony and synergy between the often oppositional attributes we have within us. Each day of *Sefirat Ha'Omer* we consciously and creatively work on another aspect of our emotional and spiritual attributes in order to correct and perfect them, establishing a state of *tikkun*. Ultimately there needs to be a blending of the attributes so that each of the seven contains all the others, so that they can operate as one unifying, healthy force in our spiritual lives. This was already practiced in the meditation — blending *Chesed* and *Gevurah* in the attribute of *Tiferet*.

After working as hard as we can on perfecting and purifying all forty-nine dimensions of our inner selves, we can hope that we are fully prepared for *Matan Torah*, the Giving of the Torah, for we have endeavored to synchronize ourselves with the forty-nine Divine attributes from which our human attributes evolved.

The renowned medieval kabbalist, Rabbi Moshe Cordovero (the Ramak), expounds upon the multiple levels of meaning to be found in the word *sefirah* (ספירה) and connects it to the *Sefirat HaOmer*. The word *sefirah* comes from the Hebrew root s-p-r.[13] This is also the root for "counting" (*lispor*), "story" (*sippur*) and "sapphire" (*sapir*). He explains that the counting should be used to create our own story, and to polish it into a luminous sapphire over the forty-nine days.[14]

---

13 In the Hebrew alphabet, the letter פ is used both as a 'p' sound (pey) and as an 'f' sound (fey).

14 Moses Cordovero, Pardes HaRimonim (The Pomegranate Orchard).

The *sefirah* of the first week of Iyar is *Tiferet*, compassion. Read the descriptions that follow, and then discuss how you can apply them in your life. Write notes for yourself in case you don't want to share your personal feelings with everyone. Writing it out will give you the ability to stand back and take an objective look at your subjective emotions. Seeing your strong and weak points will enable you to apply yourself to the development and perfection of yourself as you grow towards emotional and spiritual maturity.

The explanations that follow are taken from Simon Jacobson's *A Spiritual Guide to Counting the Omer*, published by Meaningful Life Center, NY 1996. For more on this topic, I highly recommend buying the book.

Week Three, Day One
The Chesed of Tiferet

Is my compassion tender and loving or does it come across as pity? Is my sympathy condescending and patronizing? Even if my intention is otherwise, do others perceive it as such? Does my compassion overflow with love and warmth; is it expressed with enthusiasm, or is it static and lifeless?

Week Three, Day Two
The Gevurah of Tiferet

For compassion to be effective and healthy it needs to be disciplined and focused. It requires discretion both to whom you express compassion, and in the measure of the compassion itself. It is recognizing when compassion should be expressed and when it should be withheld or limited. Discipline in compassion is knowing that being truly compassionate sometimes requires withholding compassion. Because compassion is not an expression of the bestower's needs but a response to the recipient's needs. Am I more compassionate with strangers than with close ones? If yes, why? Is the compassion coming from guilt? Does my compassion for others compromise my own needs? Am I helping others at the expense of helping myself? Perhaps the contrary is the case: Does my compassion for my family and close ones overshadow others' needs? Is my compassion impulsive and careless? Do I assess the measure of compassion necessary for a given situation? Is it commensurate with the recipient's needs? Can I possibly be hurting him with my compassion? Does my compassion overwhelm others? Is it respectful? Do I give too much or too little? Do others take advantage of my compassionate nature? When I see a needy person do I impetuously express compassion out of guilt or pity without any discretion? Do I commit the "crime" of compassion by helping him with something harmful (give him money to buy a harmful substance etc.)? Do I apply myself to determine this person's needs and help him in the best way possible?

Week Three, Day Three
The Tiferet of Tiferet

Examine the compassion of compassion. The expression of compassion and its intensity. True compassion is limitless. It is not an extension of your needs and defined by your limited perspective. Compassion for another is achieved by having a selfless attitude, rising above yourself and placing yourself in the other person's situation and experience. Am I prepared and able to do that? If not, why? Do I express and actualize the compassion and empathy in my heart? What blocks me from expressing it? Am I locked in any way? Is my compassion compassionate or self-serving? Is it compassion that comes out of guilt rather than genuine empathy? How does that affect and distort my compassion? Test yourself by seeing if you express compassion even when you don't feel guilty. Does my compassion come from a sense of duty or is it frivolous? On the other hand: Is my compassion alive; does it resound with vitality, or is it expressed only out of obligation? Is my compassion only a result of being a creature of habit who feels badly when another suffers, or do I actually apply myself to examine and refine my compassion, observing its limitations and forms of expression? How do I express compassion? Is my compassion beautiful? Is it well rounded? Does it contain the other six elements of *Tiferet*, without which my full compassion remains unrealized?

Week Three, Day Four
The *Netzach* of *Tiferet*

Is my compassion enduring and consistent? Is it reliable or whimsical? Does it prevail among other forces in my life? Do I have the capacity to be compassionate even when I'm busy with other activities or only when it's comfortable for me? Am I ready to stand up and fight for another?

Week Three, Day Five
The *Hod* of *Tiferet*

Compassion must include humility for it not to be condescending and pretentious. Hod is recognizing that my ability to be compassionate and giving does not make me better than the recipient; it is the acknowledgement and appreciation that by creating one who needs compassion G-d gave me the gift of being able to bestow compassion. Thus there is no place for haughtiness in compassion. Do I feel superior because I am compassionate? Do I look down at those that need

my compassion? Am I humble and thankful to G-d for giving me the ability to have compassion for others?

Week Three, Day Six
The *Yesod* of *Tiferet*

For compassion to be fully realized, it needs bonding. It requires creating a channel between giver and receiver. A mutuality that extends beyond the moment of need. A bond that continues to live on. That is the most gratifying result of true compassion. Do you bond with the one you have compassion for, or do you remain apart? Does your interaction achieve anything beyond a single act of sympathy?

Week Three, Day Seven
The *Malchut* of *Tiferet*

Examine the dignity of your compassion. For compassion to be complete (and enhance the other six aspects of compassion) it must recognize and appreciate individual sovereignty. It should boost self-esteem and cultivate human dignity. Both your own dignity and the dignity of the one benefiting from your compassion. Is my compassion expressed in a dignified manner? Do I manifest and emphasize majesty in my compassion? Does it elicit dignity in others? Do I recognize the fact that when I experience compassion as dignified it will reflect reciprocally in the one who receives compassion?

Kavanah for Hafrashat Challah

When the Israelites were in the desert they did not have to work for their food; their food literally fell to them from the heavens. One could say that manna was spiritual nourishment bestowed upon them so that they could devote more time to learning about God and His ways. Pray for God to help you further your quest to develop your spirituality throughout this month. Focus on this *hafrashat challah* as a springboard to reach Him.

The procedure and blessing for the *hafrashat challah* ceremony can be found on pages 14-17. Participants may wish to shape the challah afterwards, or take it home and shape it there.

SIVAN
סיוון

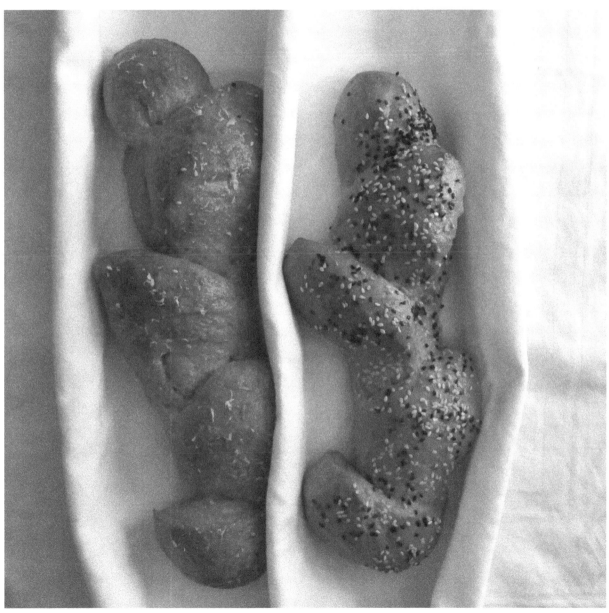

NOTE: There is an option for this months' challah to be baked dairy. There is a halachic (Jewish law) ruling that it's generally not permissible to bake dairy Challah, lest one err and eat it with a meat meal. Therefore, the *Code of Jewish Law* (Shulchan Aruch, YD 97:1) states that when baking dairy Challah, one must make it look significantly different than regular Challah, as in a different shape; bake a small amount that will likely be consumed at the meal, thereby minimizing the possibility of the leftover inadvertently get eaten with meat; and take precautions to make sure its dairy nature is clearly marked.

Wheat Stalk Challah with Parmesan Topping

Yields: 8 – 10 Stalks

INGREDIENTS

4 tablespoons active dry yeast

4 ½ cups (1.1 liters) warm water

¾ cup (150 g) organic sugar plus 2 tablespoons organic sugar

5 pounds (2.25 kg) organic white flour

1 ½ tablespoons sea salt

1 cup (230 ml) olive oil

Topping

2 cage-free organic eggs, beaten

Grated Parmesan cheese (optional)

Materials

Kitchen scissors

1 In a large bowl, combine the yeast with the 2 tablespoons of sugar and the warm water. Cover the bowl and allow the mixture to start activating. Yeast activation should take about 10 minutes; it will be bubbling and foamy.

2 Set 1 cup (125 g) of flour aside. Sift the remaining flour, sugar and salt into the bowl. Then pour oil onto the flour.

3 Combine all the ingredients, using a spatula. When it begins to form a dough, it is time to knead. At this point, you can remove the dough from the bowl and knead on the kitchen counter if it's easier for you, or directly in the bowl.

4 To knead the dough: grab the side of the dough furthest away from you and fold it toward yourself. Fold the dough in half and use your body weight to push the dough into itself. If you find that the dough is sticking too much to the surface and preventing you from kneading properly, dust the dough with flour. Give the dough a quarter turn (90 degrees). Grab the other side and fold it in half. Again, with a lot of weight behind it, push the newly folded half into itself. Repeat this process for 10-15 minutes, or until the dough is smooth, silky, elastic and the dough does not stick to the surface.

5 After the dough is thoroughly prepared, lay it on the countertop while you grease the bowl with a fine layer of oil. Next, turn the dough in the oil several times so that the dough is greased lightly on all sides.

6 Cover the bowl with a large plastic garbage bag or kitchen towel and allow it to rise for 1 hour.

7 Make the blessing on *hafrashat challah* — see **Hafrashat Challah, page 17**

8 Knead the dough again for a few more minutes and then divide the dough into 8 equal parts. Use the remaining flour for the surface area and hands to prevent sticking.

9 Roll out into logs that are about 16 inches (40 cm) long. They should look like baguettes.

10 Starting from 2 inches (5 cm) from the bottom of the dough, cut into the dough in a 45-degree angle until the depth of the cut is about ¼ inch (6 mm) from the kitchen counter. Be careful not to cut all the way through the dough. The cut will look like a V shape. Lay the piece you've cut over to one side.

11 Continue to cut into the dough, at 1 inch (2.5 cm) intervals, separating the cut pieces at opposite directions until you have reached the other end. There should be a total of 6 slits. This should look like a sheaf.

12 Cover the loaves again and let them rise in a warm place for 20 minutes.

13 If you cannot bake the challahs immediately, then this is the time to wrap the shaped dough in plastic wrap to prevent drying. You can store it in the coldest part of the refrigerator for up to 48 hours. On the day of baking, remove the dough from refrigerator and let stand on kitchen counter until it comes to room temperature, about one hour.

14 Preheat the oven to 350° F (180° C). Prepare your egg wash and decorate the top of the challah with grated Parmesan, if you want a dairy challah.

15 Bake in your preheated oven for about 25-30 minutes, or until loaves turn golden brown and shiny.

Bread should have a nice hollow sound when thumped on the bottom.

16 Remove from the oven and cool on a rack. Wait at least one hour before serving. If you are freezing the challah, wrap in waxed paper and foil. It can be stored in the freezer for up to 2 months.

Before Preparing the Dough, recite optional Rosh Chodesh Psalms, page 19.

Divine Partnership through Wheat

Today, we celebrate Shavuot primarily as the day on which the Israelites (and we, their descendants) received the Torah. The date of *Matan Torah*, however, is based on rabbinic calculations rather than any specific Godly decree; in the Torah, Shavuot is described purely as an agricultural festival. We are commanded to "hold a festival for the Feast of the Harvest, of the first fruits of your work, of what you sow in the field" (Exodus 23:16), and to "bring from your homes two loaves as a sheaf offering…they shall be of fine flour; they shall be baked with leaven; they are as first fruits to the Lord" (Leviticus 23:17). To commemorate this *mitzvah*, we are shaping our challahs as wheat stalks.

The festival is called Shavuot, which means "weeks," because the day upon which it falls is determined according to the counting of the *Omer*.[1] The *Omer* is counted for seven weeks, starting on the second day of Passover; the last day of the *Omer* is the day before Shavuot.

Shavuot is one of the three "foot" festivals, for which pilgrimages to Jerusalem were made by Jews from all over the Land of Israel. During Temple times, they were required to bring offerings — *Shtei HaLechem*, two loaves of wheat bread, as well as *bikkurim*, the first fruits of the Seven Species native to the land: wheat, barley, grapes, figs, pomegranates, olives and dates. We will be using olive oil in our challah to commemorate the *bikkurim* that our ancestors placed in beautifully decorated baskets and then carried to Jerusalem in grand

processions, joyously singing and dancing all the while, en route to the Holy Temple.

It is interesting that these offerings were of two types: one that literally comprised the first fruits of nature, the other made through human efforts. As the barley harvest ended and the wheat harvest began, God commanded that *we* complete what *He* began when he sent rain and sunshine for the crops to grow, by taking some of the most important crop and making bread from it, to offer up. Shavuot celebrates a partnership between God and His people.

Every Shavuot, for over three thousand years, we have endeavored to renew our commitment to God and to recreate these feelings of partnership. One of the customs we follow that reflects this is to eat dairy on Shavuot. There are a number of ideas as to the reason behind this tradition, of which I will offer two here. One is that the Torah, which was given on Shavuot, is likened to milk — it is complete spiritual sustenance, just as milk is complete physical sustenance for babies. Another is that until the Torah was given, the Israelites were not required to eat kosher food, but once they received it, they were. None of the meat they had in their encampment was kosher, nor were any of the pots they had used to prepare it. Since the Torah was given on Shabbat, they could not actively kosher their pots or slaughter more animals, so instead they only ate the milk and milk products they already had, since they required no preparation and were already kosher. To participate in this custom, we will be adding a Parmesan topping to our challahs, making them dairy.

As we unite for Rosh Chodesh, as our ancestors did at the foot of Mount Sinai, we anticipate the celebration of the true beginning of Jewish civilization. On the sixth of Sivan, when Shavuot begins, the moon will be just a crescent of brightness in the dark sky. Perhaps this is

---

1   See the chapter on Iyar for more details about the Counting of the Omer.

symbolic; the birth of the Jewish nation took place in darkness so that we could come into our own by our own efforts, lighting the rest of the way with *mitzvot*.

Meditation during the Kneading

The call of Sivan is to be open to receiving; open to a more profound partnership with the Divine. For any relationship to exist, both parties must come forward and participate: "That which was above came down, and that which was below climbed up" (Exodus 19:20). During Sivan, heaven and earth meet; the Divine descends and humanity rises up, creating harmony and union. This meditation is to help us become mindful of this reality.

- Start with gentle belly breathing from the nose. This allows you to have more control over your breath. Slowly inhale and exhale, pulling your breath all the way into your belly. Feel your belly expand.

- Be totally present as you slowly inhale and exhale. If your mind wanders, calmly bring it back.

- Continue to focus on your breath and just your breath. Feel the difference in temperature between how the air goes in and how it goes out.

- With each breath, open yourself to the idea of partnership with the Divine.

- Use the breath cycle as a link between two worlds — Heaven and Earth.

- Your breath and your body are intricately connected as you inhale and exhale. God gives you breath and you receive it.

- Be mindful of how you need God, and that He wants you to need Him. That is His way of partnering with you.

- Allow the spiritual power of this knowledge to filter through your heart as it travels via your kneading hands to the dough — your partnership with God. With each cycle of breathing, strengthen that reality within you.

- After the meditation, smell a fragrant spice, such as cloves, to re-involve yourself with the physical world and make you feel grounded again.

Discussion during the Rising

Ruth and Naomi — An Ideal Partnership

It is traditional to read the Book of Ruth on Shavuot for several reasons, most of which point to Ruth's exemplary behavior as a model for us. Ruth was the first official convert to the Jewish faith,[2] blazing the trail for all of us toward radical self-transformation. The inner relevance of the story of Ruth mainly stems from the quality of the core relationship it portrays. Ruth teaches us about the perfected relationship between a mother-in-law, Naomi, and a daughter-in-law, Ruth, and of their incredibly otherworldly bond.

The Book of Ruth begins with famine in Israel. To escape starvation, a family from Bethlehem — Naomi, her husband Elimelech, and their two sons, Machlon

---

2 The Torah intimates that the souls of future converts were also present at Sinai, as it says: "Neither with you only do I make this covenant and this oath; but with him that stands here with us this day before the Lord our God. And also with him that is not here with us this day" (Deuteronomy 29:13-14).

and Chilion — immigrates to Moab, a country that borders the land of Judah. Once in Moab, Elimelech dies. Naomi's sons both marry Moabite women, Ruth and Orpah. According to one midrash, Ruth and Orpah were sisters and princesses — the daughters of King Eglon of Moab.[3]

Some time later, both of Naomi's sons die, and she is left with no blood relations. Hearing that the famine in Judah is over, she decides to return to her former home in Bethlehem. Although she tells her daughters-in-law to return to their families and remarry, they both ask to accompany her to Judah. Naomi tries to dissuade them, telling them she cannot give them new husbands. Orpah is convinced to stay in Moab, but Ruth refuses. She clings to her mother-in-law and, in a famous speech, declares her eternal commitment not only to Naomi but to her people and religion: "Entreat me not to leave you, or to return from following after you: for wherever you go, I will go; and where you lodge, I will lodge: your people shall be my people, and your God my God: where you die, I will die, and there I will be buried: the Lord do so to me, and more also, if anything other than death parts us."[4] With this statement, Ruth is not only transforming herself into a source of kindness for the bereft widow, giving everything to her without reservation, she is also officially converting to Judaism.

When Naomi and Ruth arrive in Bethlehem it is harvest time. They are both worn out from their journey, and Ruth insists that Naomi rest while she goes out to the fields to see what she can find to sustain them. Ruth enters a field to glean the grain that reapers have left. It just so happens that she picks a field that belongs to Boaz, a wealthy landowner, and a relative of Naomi's.

The *midrash* relates that Boaz notices Ruth because of her modest behavior, and makes enquiries as to who she is. While the other women talk while they glean, bending over to gather the grain, she sits modestly and gleans quietly. The other women raise the hems of their garments, while she makes sure that hers remains down. The other women amuse the reapers, but Ruth turns her face away.[5]

Boaz discovers that Ruth is a Moabite, and the widowed daughter-in-law of Naomi, a relative of his. He understands that she has left her family and her country to join her fate with a people she did not previously know.[6]

Boaz approaches Ruth and tells her that she should not go to any other fields. He will make sure that she is fed, and that the reapers will not harm her. Boaz speaks to his reapers and instructs them to gather grain in such a way that Ruth will benefit from the Torah commandments regarding harvesting. Leviticus 19:9 states: "And when you reap the harvest of your land, you shall not wholly reap the corner of your field; neither shall you gather the gleaning of your harvest." The laws of *pe'ah* and *leket* were derived from this verse. *Pe'ah* means corner — the law states that when the owner of a field has his grain cut, he is to leave a corner of the field for the poor, the needy and the stranger. *Leket* means gleanings — when a reaper misses some grain with his tool, he is not allowed to go back and get it, but must leave it for the poor. Another law concerns the *shichechah*, or forgotten sheaves. When grain is taken to the granaries, some sheaves can be forgotten in the field, or dropped while they are being gathered. The Torah forbids the owner from going back and getting them; these too must be left for the poor, the widow, the orphan and the stranger.[7] Boaz tells his workers to *purposefully* drop some sheaves so that Ruth can gather them.

---

3 Ruth Rabbah 2:9
4 Ruth 1:16-17

5 Ruth Rabbah 4:9
6 Ruth 2:10-11
7 Deuteronomy 24:19

At the end of the day, Ruth returns to Naomi with a large portion of barley, and tells her everything that has happened. Naomi is happy that Ruth was so successful and found favor in Boaz's eyes, and tells Ruth that he is a kinsman. She advises Ruth to wait for Boaz at night in the threshing floor, to lie with him and seek security for herself. In *midrashic* commentary, Ruth has reservations about such an act, but nevertheless follows her mother-in-law's advice because she trusts Naomi's integrity.[8] Ultimately, Boaz marries Ruth (and does not lie with her until then). They have a son named Oved, who is the grandfather of King David.

The Book of Ruth tells an exemplary and moving tale of the love and devotion that is possible between women, even in times of sorrow and loss. It has relevance for both aspects of Shavuot; as the agricultural festival *and* the holy day that celebrates and commemorates the giving of the Torah at Sinai.

Shavuot is a harvest festival, and the *Book of Ruth* presents us with a depiction of harvest time. Moreover, the scene it paints is an ideal for us to emulate; it shows us not only the laws of *peah, leket* and *shichechah* carried out perfectly, but someone going *beyond* the letter of the law. Boaz not only ensured that the poor could gather their due in honor, he enabled Ruth to gather more than what he was actually required to give her. We witness a model of a thriving, interdependent community that lives by the Torah, and treats the poor with sympathy and love. This month is a time to rededicate ourselves to others and the deep bonds of unity that sustain us.

The harvest depicted at the end of the book is clearly a bountiful one, in contrast to the situation at the beginning of the book, when there was a famine in the land. The sages comment that famine reflects a weakening of Torah study;[9] maybe one of the reasons we read Ruth on Shavuot, the time of the Giving of the Torah, is to remind us that Torah study is a prerequisite for prosperity. Perhaps that is also one of the reasons behind the tradition of staying up all night on Shavuot to study Torah. Beyond this, and more importantly, Ruth represents the perfect convert: someone who takes upon herself the entirety of Torah voluntarily, and with love. It is appropriate for us to read about such a woman on the anniversary of the day when the Jewish people originally received and accepted the Torah, as we too were "converts" at Sinai in the wake of the Exodus from Egypt.

Ruth has a further connection to Shavuot: she was the great-grandmother of King David, who was born on Shavuot, and died on Shavuot. According to the Talmud, King David was destined to descend from Boaz and Ruth. When Boaz invited Ruth to come eat and satiate herself, he used the same language that King David used when he asked God why he had been chosen as king. The Talmud sees this connection as divinely inspired; without realizing it, Boaz was intimating to Ruth that she was worthy of siring kings.[10] It is also interesting to note that Naomi came from Bethlehem, Ruth met Boaz in Bethlehem and King David was born in Bethlehem. Bethlehem literally means "House of Bread." Bread is seen as the most elevated of foods that man can make; of all our foods, it is the only one that has a blessing all of its own. The most refined bread is made of wheat, and wheat is harvested at Shavuot time. Our most renowned, beloved king, born at the time of the wheat harvest, came from a place called "House of Bread." Maybe we can see a connection between the wheat harvest and the giving of the Torah. Bread, a symbol of royalty, can remind us of the time that we received the Torah from our King.

---

8 Ruth Rabbah 5:13; Ruth Zuta 3:2

9 Ethics of our Fathers 3:17: "Where there is no bread, there will be no Torah. Where there is no Torah, there will be no bread."

10 Talmud Shabbat 113b

The different aspects of Shavuot are all here to teach us something. When we think of it as an agricultural festival, it reminds us of the obligation of giving to the poor, even if we do not own fields and therefore do not ourselves need to observe the laws of *peah, leket* and *shichechah.* One of the ways we can give is by donating a portion of the challahs we are making today.

When we think of it as celebrating our direct relationship with God, we can commit ourselves to studying His words and laws more often, to reach a deeper understanding and connection with Him. Through charity and Torah study, we will bring unity to our people, and merit in the coming of the Messiah — the direct descendant of the righteous convert, Ruth, and her great-grandson, King David.

Reflective Questions

1. The Book of Ruth models an outstanding relationship between mother-in-law and daughter-in-law, which can be a very challenging relationship. What significance is this relationship to our receiving the Torah? What do you think we need to strive for in order to create heaven on earth?

2. How do you nurture your friendships? Do you sometimes struggle to maintain them? What are your struggles?

3. How should the relationship between daughter and mother-in-law develop so that it is based on trust, honesty and love?

4. Do you think that the Ten Commandments are the most important *mitzvot*? Why do you think there are two tablets? Do you think there is significance to that? How do the two tablets differ in commandments?

5. What do you know of the Torah views on conversion to Judaism? Do you think it should be an arduous process to convert?

6. Why is Torah study such an important part of Judaism?

7. If there is one lesson to take from the story of Ruth and Naomi, what would it be?

Kavanah for Hafrashat Challah

The classic work, *Shlah HaKadosh,*[11] contains a prayer for parents to recite for their children. It can be said at any time of the year, but especially before Shavuot, since that is when God gave us the Torah, and when the Jewish people began to be called His children. If you don't have children yourself, still focus on the blessing as it is read, since we are all God's children, and the blessing applies to all of us.

Prayer for My Children

אַתָּה הוּא ה' אֱלֹהֵינוּ עַד שֶׁלֹּא בָרָאתָ הָעוֹלָם,
וְאַתָּה הוּא אֱלֹהֵינוּ מִשֶּׁבָּרָאתָ הָעוֹלָם, וּמֵעוֹלָם
וְעַד עוֹלָם אַתָּה אֵל. וּבָרָאתָ עוֹלָמְךָ בְּגִין
לְהִשְׁתְּמוֹדְעָא אֱלָהוּתָךְ בְּאֶמְצָעוּת תּוֹרָתְךָ
הַקְּדוֹשָׁה, כְּמוֹ שֶׁאָמְרוּ רַבּוֹתֵינוּ זִכְרוֹנָם לִבְרָכָה,

---

11 Rabbi Yishayahu ben Avraham Ha-Levi (1565 — 1630), known as the Shlah, an acronym of the title of one of his major works, Shnei Luchot Ha-Brit — Two Tablets of the Covenant" was a prominent scholar of Jewish ethics, halachah and Kabbalah.

בִּי וּבְזַרְעִי וּבְזֶרַע זַרְעִי עַד עוֹלָם שׁוּם פְּסוּל
וָשֶׁמֶץ, אַךְ שָׁלוֹם וֶאֱמֶת וְטוֹב וְיָשָׁר בְּעֵינֵי
אֱלֹהִים וּבְעֵינֵי אָדָם, וְיִהְיוּ בַּעֲלֵי תוֹרָה, מָארֵי
מִקְרָא, מָארֵי מִשְׁנָה, מָארֵי תַלְמוּד, מָארֵי רָזָא,
מָארֵי מִצְוָה, מָארֵי גוֹמְלֵי חֲסָדִים, מָארֵי מִדּוֹת
תְּרוּמִיּוֹת, וְיַעַבְדוּךָ בְּאַהֲבָה וּבְיִרְאָה פְּנִימִית,
לֹא יִרְאָה חִיצוֹנִית, וְתֵן לְכָל גּוּיָה וְגוּיָה מֵהֶם דֵּי
מַחְסוֹרָהּ בְּכָבוֹד, וְתֵן לָהֶם בְּרִיאוּת וְכָבוֹד וָכֹחַ,
וְתֵן לָהֶם קוֹמָה וְיֹפִי וְחֵן וָחֶסֶד, וְיִהְיֶה אַהֲבָה
וְאַחֲוָה וְשָׁלוֹם בֵּינֵיהֶם, וְתַזְמִין לָהֶם זִוּוּגִים
הֲגוּנִים מִזֶּרַע תַּלְמִידֵי חֲכָמִים, מִזֶּרַע צַדִּיקִים,
וְגַם זִוּוּגָם יִהְיוּ כְּמוֹתָם כְּכָל אֲשֶׁר הִתְפַּלַּלְתִּי
עֲלֵיהֶם, כִּי זִכָּרוֹן אֶחָד עוֹלֶה לְכָאן וּלְכָאן

אַתָּה ה' יוֹדֵעַ כָּל תַּעֲלוּמוֹת, וּלְפָנֶיךָ נִגְלוּ
מַצְפּוּנֵי לִבִּי, כִּי כַוָּנָתִי בְּכָל אֵלֶּה לְמַעַן שִׁמְךָ
הַגָּדוֹל וְהַקָּדוֹשׁ וּלְמַעַן תּוֹרָתְךָ הַקְּדוֹשָׁה, עַל כֵּן
עֲנֵנִי ה' עֲנֵנִי, בַּעֲבוּר הָאָבוֹת הַקְּדוֹשִׁים אַבְרָהָם
יִצְחָק וְיַעֲקֹב. וּבִגְלָלָם תּוֹשִׁיעַ בָּנִים לִהְיוֹת
הָעֲנָפִים דּוֹמִים לְשָׁרְשָׁם, וּבַעֲבוּר דָּוִד עַבְדְּךָ רֶגֶל
רְבִיעִי בַּמֶּרְכָּבָה, הַמְּשׁוֹרֵר בְּרוּחַ קָדְשֶׁךָ

שִׁיר הַמַּעֲלוֹת אַשְׁרֵי כָּל יְרֵא ה' הַהֹלֵךְ בִּדְרָכָיו:
יְגִיעַ כַּפֶּיךָ כִּי תֹאכֵל אַשְׁרֶיךָ וְטוֹב לָךְ: אֶשְׁתְּךָ
כְּגֶפֶן פֹּרִיָּה בְּיַרְכְּתֵי בֵיתֶךָ בָּנֶיךָ כִּשְׁתִלֵי זֵיתִים
סָבִיב לְשֻׁלְחָנֶךָ: הִנֵּה כִי כֵן יְבֹרַךְ גָּבֶר יְרֵא ה':
יְבָרֶכְךָ ה' מִצִּיּוֹן וּרְאֵה בְּטוּב יְרוּשָׁלָ͏ִם כֹּל יְמֵי
חַיֶּיךָ: וּרְאֵה בָנִים לְבָנֶיךָ שָׁלוֹם עַל יִשְׂרָאֵל

אָנָּא ה' שׁוֹמֵעַ תְּפִלָּה יְקֻיַּם בָּנוּ הַפָּסוּק, וַאֲנִי
זֹאת בְּרִיתִי אוֹתָם אָמַר ה', רוּחִי אֲשֶׁר עָלֶיךָ

"בְּרֵאשִׁית", בִּשְׁבִיל תּוֹרָה וּבִשְׁבִיל יִשְׂרָאֵל,
כִּי הֵם עַמְּךָ וְנַחֲלָתְךָ אֲשֶׁר בָּחַרְתָּ בָּהֶם מִכָּל
הָאֻמּוֹת, וְנָתַתָּ לָהֶם תּוֹרָתְךָ הַקְּדוֹשָׁה, וְקֵרַבְתָּם
לְשִׁמְךָ הַגָּדוֹל
וְעַל קִיּוּם הָעוֹלָם וְעַל קִיּוּם הַתּוֹרָה בָּא לָנוּ מִמְּךָ
ה' אֱלֹהֵינוּ שְׁנֵי צִוּוּיִים. כָּתַבְתָּ בְּתוֹרָתְךָ "פְּרוּ
וּרְבוּ", וְכָתַבְתָּ בְּתוֹרָתְךָ "וְלִמַּדְתֶּם אֹתָם אֶת
בְּנֵיכֶם". וְהַכַּוָּנָה בִּשְׁתֵּיהֶן אַחַת, כִּי לֹא לְתֹהוּ
בְרָאתָ כִּי אִם לָשֶׁבֶת, וְלִכְבוֹדְךָ בָּרָאתָ יָצַרְתָּ אַף
עָשִׂיתָ, כְּדֵי שֶׁנִּהְיֶה אֲנַחְנוּ וְצֶאֱצָאֵינוּ וְצֶאֱצָאֵי
כָּל עַמְּךָ בֵּית יִשְׂרָאֵל יוֹדְעֵי שְׁמֶךָ וְלוֹמְדֵי תוֹרָתֶךָ

וּבְכֵן אָבֹא אֵלֶיךָ ה' מֶלֶךְ מַלְכֵי הַמְּלָכִים,
וְאַפִּיל תְּחִנָּתִי, וְעֵינַי לְךָ תְלוּיוֹת עַד שֶׁתְּחָנֵּנִי
וְתִשְׁמַע תְּפִלָּתִי לְהַזְמִין לִי בָּנִים וּבָנוֹת. וְגַם
הֵם יִפְרוּ וְיִרְבּוּ הֵם וּבְנֵיהֶם וּבְנֵי בְנֵיהֶם עַד
סוֹף כָּל הַדּוֹרוֹת, לְתַכְלִית שֶׁהֵם וַאֲנִי כֻּלָּנוּ
יַעַסְקוּ בְּתוֹרָתְךָ הַקְּדוֹשָׁה, לִלְמֹד וּלְלַמֵּד לִשְׁמֹר
וְלַעֲשׂוֹת וּלְקַיֵּם אֶת כָּל דִּבְרֵי תַלְמוּד תּוֹרָתְךָ
בְּאַהֲבָה, וְהָאֵר עֵינֵינוּ בְּתוֹרָתֶךָ וְדַבֵּק לִבֵּנוּ
בְּמִצְוֹתֶיךָ לְאַהֲבָה וּלְיִרְאָה אֶת שְׁמֶךָ

אָבִינוּ אָב הָרַחֲמָן, תֵּן לְכֻלָּנוּ חַיִּים אֲרֻכִּים
וּבְרוּכִים, מִי כָמוֹךָ אָב הָרַחֲמִים זוֹכֵר יְצוּרָיו
לְחַיִּים בְּרַחֲמִים, זָכְרֵנוּ לְחַיִּים נִצְחִיִּים, כְּמוֹ
שֶׁהִתְפַּלֵּל אַבְרָהָם אָבִינוּ "לוּ [יִשְׁמָעֵאל]
יִחְיֶה לְפָנֶיךָ," וּפֵרְשׁוּ רַבּוֹתֵינוּ זִכְרוֹנָם לִבְרָכָה,
"בְּיִרְאָתֶךָ"

כִּי עַל כֵּן, בָּאתִי לְבַקֵּשׁ וּלְחַנֵּן מִלְּפָנֶיךָ שֶׁיְּהֵא
זַרְעִי וְזֶרַע זַרְעִי עַד עוֹלָם זֶרַע כָּשֵׁר, וְאַל יִמָּצֵא

וּדְבָרַי אֲשֶׁר שַׂמְתִּי בְּפִיךָ, לֹא יָמוּשׁוּ מִפִּיךָ וּמִפִּי זַרְעֲךָ וּמִפִּי זֶרַע זַרְעֲךָ אָמַר ה' מֵעַתָּה וְעַד עוֹלָם יִהְיוּ לְרָצוֹן אִמְרֵי פִי וְהֶגְיוֹן לִבִּי לְפָנֶיךָ ה' צוּרִי וְגוֹאֲלִי

It was You, God, our God, before Creation, and it is You, God, our God, since Creation. From this world to the world to come, You are God. You created the world in order to make Your Godliness known through your holy Torah, as the sages, of blessed memory, taught: "'In the beginning...'[12] [the world was created] for the sake of Torah and for the sake of Israel," for Israel is Your nation and Your heritage. It is the nation You chose from all others, to whom You gave Your holy Torah, and which you brought close to your great Name. To insure the continuation of Your Torah, we received from You, God, our God, two commandments: You wrote in Your Torah "Be fruitful and multiply"[13] and You also wrote, "You shall teach them to your children."[14] These two commandments have a single purpose: You did not create the world so that it be desolate, but rather that it be inhabited by people; it is for Your honor that you made, created and fashioned the world, so that we, our offspring, and the offspring of all Your people, the House of Israel, know Your name and study Your Torah.

And so I come before You, God, King Who reigns over kings, and I cast my supplication before You. My eyes dependently look toward You until You will be gracious to me and hear my plea and grant me sons and daughters. And may they too be fruitful and multiply — they,

their children, and their grandchildren until the end of all generations — so that they and I might be engrossed in your holy Torah, learning, teaching, safeguarding, performing and fulfilling all the words of Your Torah's teaching with love. Enlighten our eyes in Your Torah and attach our hearts to Your commandments, to love and fear Your Name.

Our Father, merciful Father, grant us long and blessed life. Who is like You, Merciful Father, Who recalls His creatures mercifully for life? Remember us for eternal life just as Abraham our father prayed, "Oh that Yishmael might live before You!"[15] — with Fear of Heaven.

It is for this reason that I come to ask and plead before You that my children and grandchildren be upright offspring; that no blemish or imperfection be found in my children or grandchildren; that they enjoy only peace, truth and goodness; and that they may be upstanding in the eyes of God and man. May they become people of Torah, masters of Scripture, Mishna and Talmud, masters of the secrets of Torah, people of mitzvot and acts of kindness, people of sterling character, and may they serve You with love and with true, internalized fear of Heaven, not merely apparent fear. Please give each individual among my descendants all their needs in an honorable fashion. Grant them health, honor and strength, and give them stature, beauty, charm and kindness. May there be love, brotherhood and peace among them. Provide for them proper mates from families of Torah scholars and righteous God-fearing Jews. And may their mates also be blessed with everything I have asked You to grant them, since one prayer can affect the lives of many.

12 Genesis 1:1

13 Genesis 1:28

14 Deuteronomy 11:19

15 Genesis 17:18

You, God, know all deep secrets, and before You all the recesses of my heart lie bared. You know that all which I ask is for the sake of Your great and hallowed Name and for the sake of Your holy Torah. Therefore, answer me, God, please answer me, for the sake of our holy patriarchs, Abraham, Isaac and Jacob, because the forefathers assist the offspring so that they grow to be branches, which reflect their roots. Do so for the sake of King David, the fourth leg of the Holy Chariot, who sings, inspired by Your Holy Spirit.

A song of ascents. Praiseworthy is each person who fears God, who walks in His paths. When you eat the labor of your hands, you are praiseworthy, and it is well with you. Your wife shall be like a fruitful vine in the inner chambers of your home; your children shall be like olive shoots surrounding your table. Behold! For so is blessed the man who fears God. May God bless you from Zion, and may you gaze upon the goodness of Jerusalem, all the days of your life. And may you see children born to your children, peace upon Israel.[16]

Please, God, Who hears our prayers, may the words of the prophet, "'And as for Me, this is My covenant with them,' said God, 'My spirit that it upon you and My words that I have placed in your mouth shall not be withdrawn from your mouth, nor from the mouth of your offspring, nor from the mouth of your offspring's offspring,' said God, 'from this moment and forever'"[17] be fulfilled regarding me. May the expressions of my mouth and the thoughts of my heart find favor before You, God, my Rock and my Redeemer.

The procedure and blessing for the *hafrashat challah* ceremony can be found on pages 14-17. Participants may wish to shape the challah afterwards, or take it home and shape it there.

---

16 Psalms 128

17 Isaiah 59:21

TAMMUZ

תמוז

Three-Strand Carrot Raisin Challah

Yields: 8 medium challahs

INGREDIENTS

4 tablespoons active dry yeast

4 ½ cups (1.1 liters) warm water

¾ cup (150 g) organic sugar plus 2 tablespoons organic sugar

5 pounds (2.25 kg) organic white flour

1 teaspoon ground cinnamon

1 ½ tablespoons salt

½ teaspoon ground ginger

½ teaspoon ground nutmeg

1 cup (230 ml) neutral-tasting oil, such as safflower oil

1 tablespoon pure vanilla extract

2 cups (227 g) grated carrots

1 cup (150 g) raisins, soaked and drained

Topping

2 cage-free organic eggs, beaten

Cinnamon Sugar

1. In a large bowl, combine the yeast with the 2 tablespoons of sugar and the warm water. Cover the bowl and allow the mixture to start activating. Yeast activation should take about 10 minutes; it will be bubbling and foamy.

2. Set 1 cup (125 g) of flour aside. Sift the remaining flour, sugar, salt, cinnamon, ground ginger and nutmeg into the bowl.

3. Pour the oil and vanilla extract into the bowl and, with a spatula, combine all the ingredients. When it begins to form a dough, it is time to knead. At this point, you can remove the dough from the bowl and knead on the kitchen counter if it's easier for you, or directly in the bowl.

4. To knead the dough: grab the side of the dough furthest away from you and fold it toward yourself. Fold the dough in half and use your body weight to push the dough into itself. If you find that the dough is sticking too much to the surface and preventing you from kneading properly, dust the dough with flour. Give the dough a quarter turn (90 degrees). Grab the other side and fold it in half. Again, with a lot of weight behind it, push the newly folded half into itself. Repeat this process for 10-15 minutes, or until the dough is smooth, silky, elastic and the dough does not stick to the surface.

5. After the dough is thoroughly prepared, lay it on the countertop while you grease the bowl with a fine layer of oil. Next, turn the dough in the oil several times so that the dough is greased lightly on all sides.

6. Cover the bowl with a large plastic garbage bag or kitchen towel and allow it to rise for 1 hour.

7. Make the blessing on *hafrashat challah* — see *Hafrashat Challah*, page 17.

8. Knead the grated carrot and drained raisins into the dough until fully incorporated. Use the remaining flour for the surface area and hands to prevent sticking.

9 Divide the dough into 8 equal parts, and then divide each part into 3 equal logs to form the braid. Roll out the dough into even and uniform strands.

10 Lay the three strands parallel to each other. Pinch the top of the three strands together.

11 Place strand 3 over strand 2.

12 Then lay strand 1 over strand 2.

13 Then lay strand 3 over strand 2.

14 Keep on repeating until the braid is complete, and then pinch the ends together.

15 Cover the loaves again and let them rise in a warm place for 1 hour or until the dough has doubled in volume from its original size.

16 If you cannot bake the challahs immediately, then this is the time to wrap the shaped dough in plastic wrap to prevent drying. You can store it in the coldest part of the refrigerator for up to 48 hours. On the day of baking, remove the dough from refrigerator and let stand on kitchen counter until it comes to room temperature, about one hour.

17 Preheat the oven to 350° F (180° C). Brush your challahs with beaten eggs.

18 Bake in your preheated oven for about 30-35 minutes, or until loaves turn golden brown and shiny. Bread should have a nice hollow sound when thumped on the bottom.

19 Remove from the oven and cool on a rack. Wait at least one hour before serving. If you are freezing the challah, wrap in waxed paper and foil. It can be stored in the freezer for up to 2 months.

Before Preparing the Dough, recite optional Rosh Chodesh Psalms, page 19.

Correcting Sight to bring Insight

For over eight hundred years — from 833 to 423 BCE and again from 349 BCE to 69 CE — the Temple stood in Jerusalem, acting as the point of contact between God and His people. The Temple was central to the relationship between man and God, and its destruction is regarded as the greatest tragedy the Jewish people have suffered. According to tradition, the Temple will only be rebuilt for the third and final time when the Messiah comes.

For three weeks, every year, we mourn the destruction of the Temple. The period, known as the Three Weeks, or "between the straits,"[1] starts and ends with fast days. The first fast day is on the 17th of Tammuz, the day when the walls of Jerusalem were breached.[2] Three weeks later, on the 9th of Av, is the fast day commemorating the actual destruction of the Temple. We mourn not only the destruction of the Temple, but the resultant spiritual displacement, which we are still experiencing today.

This time of year has seen many more tragedies befall the Jewish people; some that were inflicted upon them, others that they caused themselves. Two that they brought upon themselves happened within a year of each other, as the people crossed the desert on their way to the Promised Land.

On Shavuot, God spoke to the Israelites, telling them the Ten Commandments, and then Moses ascended the mountain to receive the remainder of the laws. Forty days later, on the seventeenth of Tammuz, Moses came down the mountain with the Tablets of Stone, only to see the maddening sight of his people dancing around a golden calf.[3] Convinced that Moses had been away for so long that he would not return to them, they had built an idol to worship. Shocked to the core, Moses shattered the tablets.

Just a year later, Moses sent scouts into Canaan, the Promised Land,[4] to survey it. The scouts came back with a report that struck fear into the hearts of the people: "And they told him [Moses], and said: 'We came to the land where you sent us, and surely it flows with milk and honey; and this is the fruit of it. Nevertheless, the people are strong who dwell in the land, and the cities are walled and very great; and moreover we saw the children of Anak there. The Amalekites dwell in the land of the South; and the Hittites and the Jebusites and the Amorites dwell in the mountains; and the Canaanites dwell by the sea and by the coast of the Jordan....[5] We are not able to go up against the people, for they are stronger than we.' And they brought up an evil report of the land which they had searched unto the children of Israel, saying, 'The land, through which we have gone to search it, is a land that eats up its inhabitants, and all the people that we saw in it are men of great stature. And there we saw the giants, the sons of Anak, who come of the giants. And we were in our own sight as grasshoppers, and so we were in their sight' (Numbers 27-33).

---

1   Eichah Rabbah 1:29. This midrash on Eichah 1:3, "All [Zion's] pursuers overtook her between the straits," interprets "straits" as "days of distress"— namely the Seventeenth of Tammuz to the Ninth of Av.

2   During the time of the First Temple, the walls were breached on the ninth of Tammuz by Nebuchadnezzar's armies, and the fast during that time was observed on the ninth. After the destruction of the Second Temple by the Romans, when the walls were breached on the seventeenth, the fast was moved.

3   Exodus 32:19, Mishna Ta'anit 28b

4   It was always God's plan to give the land of Canaan to the descendants of Abraham: "And the fourth generation will return here, for the iniquity of the Amorites will not be complete until then" (Genesis 15:16a).

5   The Amalekites were the first enemy that the Israelites encountered after crossing the Red Sea. The Canaanites were descended from an ancestor called Canaan, the son of Ham and grandson of Noah. The Hittites, Jebusites and the Amorites were part of the original Canaanite clan that divided.

The scouts did not see the land with a positive eye, despite witnessing encouraging signs that the land was indeed plentiful and rich: for example, they brought back a cluster of grapes so enormous that two men were needed to carry it.[6] Much in life depends on perspective. They might have seen the heavily fortified Canaanite cities as a sign of weakness — Rashi points out that anyone who is truly powerful does not have to hide behind walls. Instead, they were filled with fear — only one of the scouts, Caleb, spoke with confidence of the Israelites' ability to conquer the land. Since the scouts did not see the positive element in the land of Canaan, they recommended against entering it. The people listened to them and cried out, weeping that God was setting them up for defeat. According to tradition, the night that they wept was the 9th of Av. Only Moses' pleadings on their behalf saved the people from immediate punishment; instead, God decreed that they would *not* enter the land, but would have to remain in the desert until their entire generation had died out; only their children, untainted by doubt, were truly worthy of entering the land.

In both these situations the Israelites lacked faith. Faith is the belief in something that you cannot see. This is similar to the emotional state of an infant: an infant develops an attachment with someone when they *see* them regularly. When a person to whom they are attached disappears, they become anxiety-ridden and fearful, exhibiting crankiness or even flat-out wailing. An infant cannot understand that the absent person will return; when a person is out of sight it is as though they do not exist. I believe this example explains the psychological underpinnings of the Israelites' actions; they were fearful of leaving the "cradle." God was giving the Israelites the tools to construct their own lives, by way of the Ten Commandments and a homeland, but the idea of leaving God's immediate presence and protection caused the Israelites to feel anxiety-ridden and fearful. While in the desert, they did not need to plough the earth, plant seeds, gather harvests, defend a country, run an economy, maintain a welfare system or shoulder any other earthly burdens. Essentially, they were in an infantile state, and the minute they could not *see* God they lost faith and abandoned Him. In fact, the word for fear in Hebrew is יראה (*yirah*), similar to the word for sight, ראיה (*reiyah*), which shares the same letters in Hebrew. I will venture to say that when we are consumed with *fear* it closes our channel for true *vision*.

According to **The Book of Formation**, the earliest kabbalistic text, every month in the Jewish calendar corresponds to one of the five senses. The sense that corresponds to the month of Tammuz is sight.[7] The scouts misused their sense of sight when they failed to see the good in the land, only focusing on the dangers that they perceived. Fear causes one not to see things with a positive eye.

The purpose of fasting on the 17th of Tammuz is to awaken our sense of loss over the destroyed Temple. As the full moon slowly decreases in size over the last half of the month, we begin an inward expedition into the "narrow straits." We must work to transcend the fear that causes us to see things with a negative eye. We need to train ourselves to see when we cannot see.

To demonstrate our commitment to seeing wisely and positively, we are baking Carrot Raisin Challah. Carrots are high in vitamin A, a nutrient that is essential for good vision. This month we will amend the negative use of our eyesight, looking at challenges or hardships with courage, patience, trust and optimism. The raisins in the challah allude to the sweetness of our potential to indeed see positively. Each Rosh Chodesh carries within it the buds of repair and newness, even Tammuz, the month when we enter the straits of our national tragedies. As the moon blossoms, so should our inner eye and faith.

---

6 Numbers 13:23

7 Sefer Yetzirah (The Book of Formation) 5:1

We will shape our loaves into three-strand braided challahs. The shape this creates is reminiscent of the Hebrew letter *Shin*, which we will be focusing on during our visualization meditation this month. Since braids don't appear in nature, but are created by humans, using them for our challahs is a way to recognize that we have the ability to use our creativity to bring God closer to us.

Meditation during Kneading

An important discipline in meditation is learning how to control images in the mind's eye when your eyes are closed. When you have learned how to do this, you can also learn how to *hold* an image in your mind's eye. This technique is known as visualization, and it facilitates the opening of your senses to the perception of higher-dimensional worlds and energies, beyond those that one actually physically sees.

A simple way to begin learning this discipline is through visualizing a letter. We will visualize the Hebrew letter *Shin* in our mind's eye. Although you can use any letter to meditate upon, I have chosen *Shin* because its shape mimics the structure of the bottom section of the human heart. In the *Shema* we are instructed to *listen*, by way of opening up our perceptions so that we can inscribe God's commandments on our *hearts*.[8] The ultimate goal of this visualization is to draw down spiritual energy through gaining control of our mental images.

- Start with gentle belly breathing from the nose. This allows you to have more control over your breath. Slowly inhale and exhale, pulling your breath all the way into your belly. Feel your belly expand.

- Be totally present as you slowly inhale and exhale. If your mind wanders, calmly bring it back.

- Continue to focus on your breath and just your breath. Feel the difference in temperature between how the air goes in and how it goes out.

- Once you feel yourself enter a meditative state, close your eyes, and direct your thoughts to the letter *Shin*, in the color black. Just relax and allow the image to gently settle in your mind's eye.

- Try to see the letter exactly how you saw it with your eyes open.

- Concentrate on the *Shin*, try to fix it in your inner visual field.

- If the *Shin* gets disrupted with other images, you may repeat the word *Shin*, over and over. Use the knead to release wandering thoughts into the dough, so that your mind can focus.

- Once you are able to lock the image in your mind's eye, engrave the *Shin* on your inner visual field: imagine white fire burning around the letter.

- This white fire inscribes the Divine within you. God is always with you, even if you can't see Him.

After the meditation, smell a fragrant spice such as cloves to re-involve yourself with the physical world, and make you feel grounded again.

---

8 Deuteronomy 6:6

In future, you can access this meditation to develop the visualization method. The more you do it, the easier it will be to hew away at extraneous imagery and just focus on one image — a positive image seen with a positive eye.

Discussion during the Rising

Seeing with the Inner Eye

The names of all the months in the Hebrew calendar are originally from Babylon. The Jewish people adopted these Babylonian names during the seventy-year exile in Babylon.

Tammuz was the name of a Sumerian fertility god adopted by the Babylonians, symbolizing the fertilization of nature for the coming year.[9] Every year, the Tammuz cult would mourn the death of Tammuz at the beginning of the summer solstice. The Babylonians marked the decline in daylight hours and the onset of "killing" summer heat and drought with a six-day "funeral" for the god, marking the end of the natural powers of fertility.[10] The Israelite women adopted this idolatrous custom, also mourning over Tammuz, wailing at the gate of the Temple: "He brought me to the entrance of the north gate to the Lord's house; and there before me were women weeping for Tammuz."[11]

The prophet Ezekiel, exiled to Babylon before the destruction of the Temple, forewarned that it would be destroyed if the people refused to repent of worshipping pagan gods, but his warnings fell on deaf ears. Idolatry was too attractive a lure. Tragically, on the 9th of Tammuz the walls around Jerusalem were breached by Nebuchadnezzar's armies, and the Temple service was disrupted. The Temple was destroyed a month later, on the 9th of Av.

The Jews made the same mistake that their ancestors did as they waited for Moses to come down from Sinai. Not being able to see him, fearing that he was gone forever, they turned to the worship of an idol that they could see. Thousands of years later, the people defied their priests and leaders and turned to idolatry again, worshipping Tammuz and other pagan gods. They wanted to *see* their gods; they could only believe if they had a tangible idol to focus on. We shouldn't believe everything we see. When our eyes are left to their own devices, they can easily be tricked and drawn towards the desires of the heart, as it says in the Torah, "Do not turn after your heart and after your eyes" (Numbers 15:39). This is a warning to be on constant guard not to let your eyes lead you in the wrong direction. Even in the darkness of the night sky we need to find the inner light that we engraved on our mind's eye to exercise our sight in the most positive way possible.

When we turn our eyes towards spirituality they can lead us in the right direction. "Lift up your eyes to the heavens, and see who created these [stars]" (Isaiah 40:26). If we look at the stars, we can see God's handiwork and come to know Him by raising our thoughts above the earth, fixing our attention on the works of God in distant planets; in the number, the order, the greatness and the harmony of the heavenly bodies. Ecclesiastes echoes this advice with "A wise man has eyes in his head" (2:14). God created the world in a way that leads us towards Him, if we *look* at it properly. When we see the beauty, the majesty and the awesomeness of the universe we can't help but be drawn to God. God told us to "choose

---

9 Bromiley, Geoffrey W. International Standard Bible Encyclopedia: Q-Z pg. 86

10 Ibid., p. 87

11 Ezekiel 8:14

life" (Deuteronomy 30:19). But to choose life, one needs to be able to *see* the goodness in life and to engage it. Perhaps that is another reason why the sense of the month is sight.

In Hebrew, the term for idolatry is *avodah zarah*, which literally translates as "strange work." Baking challah on Rosh Chodesh, and separating it as we were commanded, is the antithesis of idolatry. It affirms our commitment to seeing God's role in our lives correctly.

Reflective Questions

1. After all the miracles God performed for the Israelites upon the Exodus from Egypt, why do you think they lost faith so quickly? Whenever something did not go as they expected, they were ready to abandon God. Can you understand this? How do you think you would feel?

2. How do you think you would feel if God spoke to you directly, and told you that you had a special function in the world?

3. How does God offering the Promised Land to the Israelites compare to a child growing up and leaving home? Why would a child not want to leave home?

4. The twelve scouts were the heads of the twelve tribes of Israel; they must have had the best of intentions. Can you blame them for their evil report? Why do you think they spoke out in the way they did?

5. How will you exercise "seeing" with a positive eye? What steps do you think you can take to facilitate this endeavor?

Kavanah for Hafrashat Challah

Experiencing pain or sorrow during the Three Weeks could be a prompt from God for some soul-searching, or a change in direction. Ask God that he help you be able to "see" in the most positive way possible, so that your inner sight may be rectified.

The procedure and blessing for the *hafrashat challah* ceremony can be found on pages 14-17. Participants may wish to shape the challah afterwards, or take it home and shape it there.

Three-Ringed Chocolate Challah

Yields: 8 challahs

INGREDIENTS

4 tablespoons active dry yeast

4 ½ cups (1.1 liters) warm water

¾ cup (150 g) organic sugar plus 2 tablespoons organic sugar

5 pounds (2.25 kg) organic white flour

1 cup (118 grams) fair-trade cocoa powder or

6-ounces (170 g) vegan chocolate chips

1 ½ tablespoons sea salt

1 cup (230 ml) neutral-tasting oil, such as safflower oil

Topping

2 cage-free organic eggs, beaten

Cocoa sugar (equal parts cocoa and sugar)

1 In a large bowl, combine the yeast with the 2 tablespoons of sugar and the warm water. Cover the bowl and allow the mixture to start activating. Yeast activation should take about 10 minutes; it will be bubbling and foamy.

2 Set 1 cup (125 g) of flour aside. Sift the flour, cocoa powder, sugar, and salt into the bowl.

3 Pour the oil onto the flour. Combine all the ingredients, using a spatula. When it begins to form a dough, it is time to knead. At this point, you can remove the dough from the bowl and knead on the kitchen counter if it's easier for you, or directly in the bowl.

4 To knead the dough: grab the side of the dough furthest away from you and fold it toward yourself. Fold the dough in half and use your body weight to push the dough into itself. If you find that the dough is sticking too much to the surface and preventing you from kneading properly, dust the dough with flour. Give the dough a quarter turn (90 degrees). Grab the other side and fold it in half. Again, with a lot of weight behind it, push the newly folded half into itself. Repeat this process for 10-15 minutes or until the dough is smooth, silky, and elastic and does not stick to the surface.

5 After the dough is thoroughly prepared, lay it on the countertop while you grease the bowl with a fine layer of oil. Next, turn the dough in the oil several times so that the dough is greased lightly on all sides.

6 Cover the bowl with a large plastic garbage bag or kitchen towel and allow it to rise for 1 hour.

7 Make the blessing on *hafrashat challah* — see **Hafrashat Challah, page 17.**

8 Mix in the chocolate chips, if using. Knead the dough again for a few more minutes and then divide the dough into 8 equal parts. Use the remaining flour for the surface area and hands to prevent sticking.

9 Further divide each part into 3 equal logs. Roll each portion into a long strand. Form a circle with 1 strand by pinching the ends together to look like a bagel.

10 Loop the other 2 strands through the middle circle and join their ends by pinching together to form 2 new circles. Conceal the joined seams by hiding them under the overlapping dough. The end result should look similar to the Olympic symbol.

11 Cover the loaves again and let them rise in a warm place for 1 hour or until the dough has doubled in volume from its original size. Pinch the seams again firmly in place, so it does not open during baking.

12 If you cannot bake the challahs immediately, then this is the time to wrap the shaped dough in plastic wrap to prevent drying. You can store it in the coldest part of the refrigerator for up to 48 hours. On the day of baking, remove the dough from refrigerator and let stand on the kitchen counter until it comes to room temperature, about one hour.

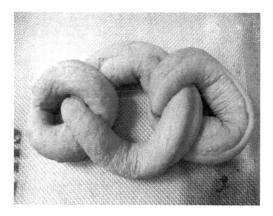

13 Preheat the oven to 350° F (180° C). Glaze with egg wash and sprinkle with cocoa sugar if desired.

14 Bake in your preheated oven for about 25-30 minutes, or until loaves turn dark brown and shiny. Bread should have a nice hollow sound when thumped on the bottom.

15 Remove from the oven and cool on a rack. Wait at least one hour before serving. If you are freezing the challah, wrap in waxed paper and foil. It can be stored in the freezer for up to 2 months.

Before Preparing the Dough, recite optional Rosh Chodesh Psalms, page 19.

Introduction to Challah Theme during the Yeast Activation

Man, Woman and God

The first nine days of Av see an intensification of the mourning period that began with the fast day of the Seventeenth of Tammuz and ends with the fast day of the Ninth of Av. During these three weeks, our greatest national tragedies took place — most importantly, the destruction of both the First and the Second Temples. The sacrificial offerings that were made in the Temples maintained the Jewish People in 'good health' and enabled us to receive God's Divine influence. The fire of the sacrifices united the Divine Presence with the physical world.[1] The destruction of the Temple meant the loss of a direct connection with God.

A mere six days after the sadness of Tisha B'Av, however, comes the joyous holiday of the fifteenth of Av. Tu B'Av, a holiday that went uncelebrated for many centuries, has been rejuvenated in recent decades, especially in Israel. In modern times, it has become the Israeli Valentine's Day, celebrated as the day of love. During Temple times it was a minor holiday celebrating the wood offering[2] brought to the Temple, as well as the beginning of the grape harvest. Unmarried girls would dress in white and go out to dance in the vineyards, where bachelors could find them and declare their interest.[3] In a sort of romantic masquerade,

the girls would lend white clothing to one another so that their prospects would not know who could afford expensive dresses, and who was only borrowing them. To my mind, this practice was encouraging the maidens of the land to show unconditional *chesed* (lovingkindness) towards each other, mirroring one of God's own attributes.[4] *Chesed* is a link in a chain, connecting people to personal involvement and commitment to further social change.

The Second Temple was destroyed, we are taught, because of the baseless hatred felt by Jews for each other. The Temple will only be rebuilt when we commit to the opposite: boundless love. This is the connection we can make between the two days we are marking this month: Tisha B'Av and Tu B'Av. Perhaps by working to create and build loving interpersonal relationships that unite, we will make ourselves worthy of the rebuilding of the Temple. To enhance our feelings of love on Tu B'Av, we are making chocolate challah, since chocolate has long been associated with love. In fact, chocolate increases endorphins and serotonin — the feel-good brain chemicals that enhance mind and mood.

We will shape the challah into three rings, which will carry a double weight of meaning to reflect the two days we are honoring. On the one hand, the three-ringed challah marks the tragedies of Tisha B'Av by expressing a hope for unity; for the reconnection of self, nation and God. Tradition holds that the Messiah will come on the Ninth of Av and turn a day of mourning into one of celebration and joy; the three-ringed challah reminds us of the unity we must build in order for that day to come. On the other hand, the three rings can also express the interlinking of self with partner, together with God — what we hope happens when we marry. We celebrate the perpetuation of Jewish life that comes with finding a suitable partner and building a home together; one that is mindful of a connection with God.

---

1 Kuzari 2:26 — 2:29

2 After the Babylonian exile, Ezra and Nechemiah came to rebuild the First Temple but found the land desolate and all the trees uprooted by the enemy. They needed wood for the altar offerings, and contributions of wood came to be known as "wood offerings." These offerings were celebratory events, similar to first fruit offerings. After this time it became forbidden to cut down trees for use in the Temple fires (Ta'anit 31a). Wood used to fuel the altar had to be entirely dried out, but after Tu B'Av the days become shorter, which meant there would not be enough sunlight to dry out freshly-cut logs. By this date, therefore, all the cutting of the wood for the altar had to be completed and the supply was complete until the next summer.

4 The Thirteen Attributes of Mercy are enumerated in Exodus 34:6-7, and are the attributes through which God governs the world.

So, for Tisha B'Av, the three-ringed challah symbolizes the self, the nation and God; and for Tu B'Av, the self, the partner and God. Interlinking the rings suggests the unifying force that brings a synthesis to the whole.

Meditation during Kneading

We are all drawn to the familiar, the secure, the habits and routines of everyday life. Sometimes we shy away from expanding our horizons because it is scary to take a risk for the sake of the unknown. Committing to a lifetime partner requires that we take some risk, not only before marriage, but during the marriage as well.

The word *echad*, one, has the same numerical value as the word *ahava*, love. Love has the power to break down barriers and unify opposites, joining them in oneness. In the Torah, oneness refers to God's unity.[5] Love gives you the ability to expand yourself and intensify your relationship with your partner, and with God. This meditation is about making room for a partner in your life — whether it is a partner you already have, or one that you hope to have. It is also about opening your heart and expanding.

- Begin with gentle belly breathing from the nose. This allows you to have more control over your breath. Slowly inhale and exhale, pulling your breath all the way into your belly. Feel your belly expand.

- Be totally present as you slowly inhale and exhale. If your mind wanders, calmly bring it back.

- Continue to focus on your breath and just your breath. Feel the difference in temperature between how the air goes in and how it goes out.

- Once you feel yourself enter a meditative state, intentionally breathe in very slowly — breathing in renewal.

- Exhale from your mouth, longer than your inhalation, imagining that you are breaking through boundaries — expanding yourself to make room.

- Again inhale, breathing in *A-H-A-V-A*, love. Feel it enter from the crown of your head, and wash over you all the way down to your toes.

- Exhale from your mouth. Feel the *A-H-A-V-A* expand from your kneading hands into the challah.

- The challah, being a part of you, is part of something greater — whether part of a loving couple, the comradeship of this group, or your relationship with God. You are one. You are *A-H-A-V-A*.

After the meditation is complete, smell a fragrant spice such as cloves to re-involve yourself with the physical world, and help you feel grounded again.

---

5   An example of this is in the Shema prayer, where we state "God is One." It means not only that there is one God, but that God and the whole of creation are one — there is nothing apart from God.

Expansion

During the Three Weeks leading up to Tisha B'Av, there are no weddings, parties or public celebrations, and people are expected to refrain from going to concerts or listening to music. It is forbidden to get haircuts or for men to shave. During the first nine days of Av, an even stricter level of mourning is observed, following the Talmudic dictum: "When the month of Av begins, we reduce our joy."[6] We abstain from foods traditionally associated with joy, such as wine and meat, except on Shabbat. Bathing, beyond what is absolutely necessary, is prohibited, as is doing laundry, and buying or wearing new clothes.[7] These mourning rituals are supposed to help us banish the distractions we experience on ordinary days, and remove any outer trappings of "normality," so that we focus on what is important. When we are left with just our thoughts in the darkness left by the Rosh Chodesh moon, we are pushed into a place where we have to be reflective. There is nowhere to turn but inwards. The intensity of mourning reaches its peak on the fast of Tisha B'Av.

The Talmud describes the period of the Second Temple as a time when people were occupied with Torah and keeping the commandments, yet there was an extremely serious and pervasive problem that nullified this worthy Torah focus: baseless hatred.[8] Although the people were following the letter of the law, they missed the essential spirit of the law — to live a life of Torah for the sake of loving their fellow man. The land was rife with conflict between neighbors, between different elements of the community. This is why the Temple was destroyed. Rav Kook, the first chief rabbi of Israel, wrote in one of his most often-quoted statements: "If we were destroyed, and the world with us, due to baseless hatred, then we shall rebuild ourselves, and the world with us, with baseless love — *ahavat chinam*."[9] During this time of sadness and mourning for what was and what could have been, we should be thinking about how to correct this fault: how we, today, can give love to others. We must work on expanding ourselves, and our hearts. We must accept others as they are with their limitations, because no one is perfect. We must accept that we were created with individually distinctive personalities and characteristics, in order to contribute a unique piece of ourselves that enhances our colorful Jewish nation. Each one of us counts!

In ancient times, on Tu B'Av, the daughters of Jerusalem sought out love by boldly dancing in the vineyards, waiting to be courted. There is something very sensual about dancing in a vineyard: vineyards can represent fertility, and the desire to multiply in abundance. In fact, a cluster of grapes is similar in shape to the uterus. The grapes that were harvested during the festival of Tu B'Av would be used to make wine, which is always used in Judaism for sanctification and to infuse holiness *(kedusha)* into our lives, including during the wedding service. The Mishna explains that the women would say, "Young man, lift up your eyes and choose wisely. Don't look only at physical beauty, look rather at the family, 'For charm is false, and beauty is vain. A God-fearing woman is the one to be praised...'"[10] Essentially, the women in the fields were saying that shared Jewish

---

6 Babylonian Talmud, Tractate Ta'anit 26b

7 The different levels of mourning given here are according to the Ashkenazi custom. Sephardim do not have a three week period of mourning; they begin only on the first of Av, and the extra intensity of mourning is expected only during the actual week during which Tisha B'Av falls.

8 Talmud Yoma 9b

9 Rabbi Abraham Isaac Kook, Orot HaKodesh (Holy Lights) vol. III, p.324

10 Mishna Ta'anit 4:8. The quote within the Mishna is from Proverbs 31:30. Today this phrase is part of the "Eshet Chayil" hymn that a husband sings to his wife before *Kiddush* on Friday night. The hymn is a song of praise for all the woman of the house has done for him and their family throughout the week.

values serve serve to help a relationship bloom, not external beauty. Beauty comes from within, and if you really want a meaningful relationship, you need to encourage your prospective match's soul to rise up, so you can discover their essence.

We all need to break through external barriers in order for love to grow. We need to build and sustain relationships in which we give selflessly, always seeing the good in the other and supporting them with kind words and deeds. The kindness and love that are present in such a loving, Torah-based relationship is a fine exemplar of the lovingkindness we need to show *all* people.[11]

Moreover, when love is actualized through marriage, it is, in essence, creating a microcosm of the Sanctuary (the precursor to the Temple). The Talmud says that every person is like a mini-world.[12] With this in mind, let us look at what God said when He charged the Israelites with building a Sanctuary: "And let them make Me a Sanctuary, that I may dwell among them" (Exodus 25:8). The world needed a Sanctuary for God, but once it was built, He would dwell among *them*, not *it*. The sanctuary was a conduit, a tool, not an actual residence, that gave God a way to dwell among His people. Today we have no Sanctuary, no Temple, but there can still be a way to actualize this commandment. If we regard every person as a world in and of themselves, then every person needs to build a sanctuary for God within themselves — in

their hearts, as a place for the Divine presence to dwell. I propose that the plural command, "among them" may also suggest that this sanctuary in our hearts is *best* built within the physical union of marriage. The Talmud says that if a husband and wife dwell together in peace and harmony, the *Shechinah* will abide with them and fill their home with an atmosphere of holiness.[13] Tu B'Av can therefore be viewed as a holiday that honors love for God by (re)establishing a truly loving relationship with a spouse.

Av, in Hebrew, means father. If we take the month as such, then we have to say that the beginning of the month starts with our Father disappointed in us. But by the time the full moon is shining, He is rejoicing with us as we turn our focus from the sadness of disunity and destruction to the joy of reunion and marriage. Tisha B'Av and Tu B'Av are reflective of the process of estrangement and reunion; if Tisha B'Av represents an estrangement from our better selves and from God, then Tu B'Av represents the ultimate reunion — of two halves of a soul joined together in marriage, and the joy that comes after taking the necessary risks for expansion.

Reflective Questions

1. What does the Temple mean to you?

2. Has there been a time when you lost the best thing that you had? Why do you think you lost it? Were you in any way responsible?

3. What areas of faith need expansion in your life?

4. How do you relate to Tisha B'Av? If you have never felt it to be relevant to you before, do you think differently now?

---

11 "Go forth, O ye daughters of Zion, and gaze upon King Solomon, even upon the crown wherewith his mother hath crowned him on the day of his wedding, and on the day of the gladness of his heart" (Song of Songs 3:11). "On the day of his wedding": This refers to the day of the giving of the Law. "And on the day of the gladness of his heart": this refers to the building of the Temple; which alludes to the fact that through marriage there is the potential for the rebuilding of the Temple. (Babylonian Talmud, Tractate Ta'anit 4:8)

12 "For this reason was Adam created alone: To teach us that whoever destroys a single soul, the Torah regards as guilty as though he had destroyed an entire world; and whoever preserves a single soul the Torah ascribes merit to him as though he had preserved an entire world." Babylonian Talmud, Sanhedrin 37a.

13 Babylonian Talmud, Sotah 17a.

5. Do you relate to Tu B'Av? If you never have before, do you think it will be different now?

6. How do you define a loving relationship? Does your definition outline the success of your own relationship with your significant other?

7. What drew you to your significant other? What qualities do you find attractive in a man?

8. What qualities do you think are essential for a successful relationship? If you are married, has your opinion on these qualities changed since you got married, or do they still hold true for you now?

9. What advice would you give on love and marriage to a younger version of yourself?

Kavanah for Hafrashat Challah

Love has the ability to heal and unify the world — but it takes courage to risk your heart in the search for love. Ask God to give you courage to reach exponential growth — whether married or not, we sometimes need to take risks for our true potential to manifest.

The procedure and blessing for the *hafrashat challah* ceremony can be found on pages 14-17. Participants may wish to shape the challah afterwards, or take it home and shape it there.

ELUL

אלול

Crown-shaped Challah with Olive Oil and Za'atar

Yields: 8 medium challahs

INGREDIENTS

4 tablespoons active dry yeast

4 ½ cups (1.1 liters) warm water

¾ cup (150 g) organic sugar plus 2 tablespoons organic sugar

5 pounds (2.25 kg) organic white flour

1 ½ tablespoons sea salt

1 cup (230 ml) olive oil

Topping

Extra Virgin Olive oil, for glaze

Coarse sea salt

Za'atar

1. In a large bowl, combine the yeast with the 2 tablespoons of sugar and the warm water. Cover the bowl and allow the mixture to start activating. Yeast activation should take about 10 minutes; it will be bubbling and foamy.

2. Set 1 cup (125 g) of flour aside. Sift the remaining flour, sugar and salt into the bowl.

3. Pour the oil onto the flour. Combine all the ingredients, using a spatula. When it begins to form a dough, it is time to knead. At this point, you can remove the dough from the bowl and knead on the kitchen counter if it's easier for you, or directly in the bowl.

4. To knead the dough: grab the side of the dough furthest away from you and fold it toward yourself. Fold the dough in half and use your body weight to push the dough into itself. If you find that the dough is sticking too much to the surface and preventing you from kneading properly, dust the dough with flour. Give the dough a quarter turn (90 degrees). Grab the other side and fold it in half. Again, with a lot of weight behind it, push the newly folded half into itself. Repeat this process for 10-15 minutes, or until the dough is smooth, silky, elastic and the dough does not stick to the surface.

5. After the dough is thoroughly prepared, lay it on the countertop while you grease the bowl with a fine layer of oil. Next, turn the dough in the oil several times so that the dough is greased lightly on all sides.

6. Cover the bowl with a large plastic garbage bag or kitchen towel and allow it to rise for 1 hour.

7. Make the blessing on *hafrashat challah* — see **Hafrashat Challah, page 17.**

8. Knead the dough again for a few more minutes. Use the remaining flour, for the surface area and hands to prevent sticking.

9. Divide the dough into 24 equal parts and roll out each part into even and uniform strands.

10. Arrange 4 strands in front of you, tic-tac-toe style. There should be 2 sets of 2 strands where the strands are one under and one over in each set. This should form a woven cross. Each of the parallel pairs has a strand that's an "over" and a strand that's an "under."

11 Starting in a counter clockwise rotation, in each parallel pair, cross the under over the "over." So, in the top pair, cross the right over the left forming a 90° degree angle. Continue until you have completed one rotation. The old "overs" are now "unders" and have not moved. There are now 4 new sets of pairs; line each pair up in parallel lines as best as you can. In a clockwise direction, repeat with all four pairs.

12 If you still have some room on the strands, continue weaving, switching directions with each round.

13 To finish, pinch each set of two ends together firmly, then bring all four sets together towards the center. Carefully flip over your challah and you will have a beautiful, woven, round challah.

14 Line a baking sheet with wax paper, and leave to rise on the baking sheet. Cover the challahs loosely with plastic wrap and let rise for 40 minutes.

15 f you cannot bake the challah immediately, then this is the time to wrap the shaped dough in plastic wrap to prevent drying. You can store it in the coldest part of the refrigerator for up to 48 hours. On the day of baking, remove from refrigerator and let stand on kitchen counter until it reaches room temperature, about 1 hour.

16 Preheat the oven to 350° F (180° C). Glaze the challahs with olive oil, sprinkle with toppings and bake according to recipe instructions.

17 Bake in your preheated oven for about 30-35 minutes, or until loaves turn golden brown and shiny. Bread should have a nice hollow sound when thumped on the bottom.

18 Remove from the oven and cool on a rack. Wait at least one hour before serving. If you are freezing the challah, wrap in waxed paper and foil. It can be stored in the freezer for up to 2 months.

Before Preparing the Dough, recite optional Rosh Chodesh Psalms, page 19.

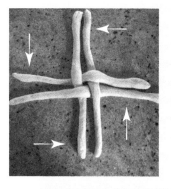

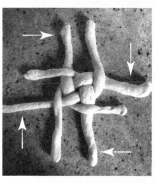

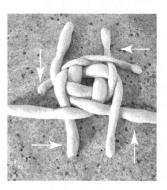

Introduction to Challah Theme during the Yeast Activation

God is in the Field

Elul, the last month of the Hebrew year, is also the month preceding the high holidays — Rosh Hashanah (the New Year) and Yom Kippur (the Day of Atonement). In Jewish tradition, the New Year is a time when we are judged by God for our actions over the previous year. In Elul, we prepare for the Day of Judgment (Rosh Hashanah) and the sealing of that judgment (Yom Kippur) by auditing our spiritual accounts and assessing the year gone year gone by through a process known as *teshuvah*. We take courage in this spiritual introspection, knowing that Elul is a time of particular closeness to God.[1]

The founder of Chabad Chasidism, the Alter Rebbe, described God's position during the month of Elul as that of "the king in the field." Usually, the king's place is in his capital city, in the royal palace. Anyone who wishes to approach him must do so through specific channels, via official requests and lengthy bureaucratic procedures. They must prepare what they wish to say in advance, and their dress and manner must be appropriate for a palace visit. However, sometimes the king comes out to the fields outside the city. Anyone can approach him; the king receives all his subjects, smiling and gracious, just as they are. This is God during the month of Elul. He is drawn out of "concealment" and approachable. Everyone works in the field — the "field" represents the entire spectrum of our workday endeavors, as we all labor for "bread." Most of our lives are spent "tilling the land," be it in offices, in wheat fields or in the kitchen, baking bread. When God seems more approachable, the process of *teshuvah* can be no mere cerebral reflection,

but a spiritual awakening and transformation of the soul. Shaping our challahs into crowns is our way to mark this special time.

To ignite this process of spiritual awakening, we are baking challah on Rosh Chodesh Elul as the vehicle for transformation. As we sift flour from the "field," we can think about separating out the obstacles that block us from coming closer to God. I have suggested the use of olive oil in this month's recipe for two reasons. One, olive oil is more holy than other oils since it is regarded as a characteristic product from the Land of Israel. Its intrinsic superiority made it part of the burnt offering in Temple times. Second, it was used to treat wounds and heal the sick, as seen in the verse in Isaiah: "From the sole of the foot even to the head, there is no soundness in it, but bruises and sores and raw wounds; they are not pressed out or bound up or softened with oil" (1:6).

So, we pour olive oil into the flour to soften the harm we have done ourselves by giving in to our faults and limitations, using it as a healing balm that will allow us to grow stronger and renew us. As the oil joins with the flour to create a soft dough, we can search our hearts, gently, contemplating whether we have made the most of our lives during the past year. We use our hands to create the "staff of life" while directing our thoughts to the king in the field, who is awaiting our penitence.

Historically, salt has been used for purity and consecration, and was always used with sacrifices. Salt is also a symbol of permanence, making it a suitable topping for the month of Elul, when we are seeking to recommit to our perpetual and everlasting covenant with God. Hyssop was another herb seen as purifying, and used in many rituals and sacrifices. Today it is an ingredient in the herb mixture known as *za'atar,* another suitable topping for Elul, when we are seeking to purify our souls.

1 Rabbi Shneur Zalman of Liadi, Likkutei Torah, Re'eh 32b

Meditation during Kneading

In addition to special Selichot services (penitential prayers) recited during Elul, Psalm 27 is read twice a day. Ashkenazim add it to the morning and evening prayer services, while Sephardim add it to morning and afternoon services. While the complete psalm will be read during the rising of the challah, it is appropriate to focus on one particular verse of the psalm for the meditation:

> *One thing I ask of God, one thing I request:*
> *To dwell in the house of God all the days of my life*
> *To behold God's graciousness, and to visit in His*
> *palace. (Psalm 27:4)*

On the surface, David's plea is that he be allowed to spend all his time in the Holy Temple. Rabbi Shimshon Raphael Hirsch[2] elaborated on this passage by suggesting that David is expressing a different, much deeper idea: "Dwelling in the house of God cannot mean a physical dwelling in the actual House of the Lord. Even the priests were not constantly in the Temple. The phrase rather describes that conception of life and of the fulfillment of its duties which can make of any place a Divine sanctuary...."[3] If we sanctify our lives, if we develop spiritual attentiveness, then we can experience the entire world — every place we find ourselves, and every activity that we engage in — as God's home, God's palace. It is a dimension of being that anyone can enter, if they work at it. King David strove to be in that state of being, and so can we.

Striving to increase our connection to the infinite is vital at all times, but during the month of Elul it can be a form of repentance: we show God that we are mindful of His universe and, therefore, we intend to take more precaution in protecting our words, our thoughts and our actions.

- Start with gentle belly breathing from the nose. This allows you to have more control over your breath. Slowly inhale and exhale, pulling your breath all the way into your belly. Feel your belly expand.

- Be totally present as you slowly inhale and exhale. If your mind wanders, calmly bring it back.

- Continue to focus on your breath and just your breath. Feel the difference in temperature between how the air goes in and how it goes out.

- Once you feel yourself enter a meditative state, direct your thoughts to the verse, "*One thing I ask of God, one thing I request: To dwell in the house of God all the days of my life. To behold God's graciousness, and to visit in His palace.*"

- Concentrate on the meaning of the verse, allowing the spiritual power of your request to filter through your mind and heart as it travels via your kneading hands to the dough.

- Focus on one aspect of closeness to the Divine that you think would be easiest to implement, or that would mean most to you. Pray for it.

- Use the knead to focus on this request. Stay focused on it while you knead the dough.

After the meditation is complete, smell a fragrant spice such as cloves to re-involve yourself with the physical world and help you feel grounded again.

---

2 Rabbi Shimshon Rafael Hirsch, 1808-1888, is considered by many to be the father of Modern Orthodox Judaism. He was a fiery leader, brilliant writer, and profound educator.

3 The Hirsch Psalms Feldheim Publishers, Jerusalem/New York, p194

Search Inside your Heart

Think of the challah dough rising as a metaphor for our ability to rise from difficult situations by learning from them. There is a hint of sweetness in even the bitterest experiences if we can turn them to good.

Since ancient times, the month of Elul has been a time of reconciliation between God and Israel. Moses went up Mount Sinai to receive the Torah during the month of Sivan, but his return with the Ten Commandments was marred by the people's sin with the Golden Calf, and the tablets were destroyed. Tradition holds that the day Moses ascended Mount Sinai for the second time, to plead for forgiveness for his people, was Rosh Chodesh Elul. He descended, with God's forgiveness and a new set of *Luchot HaBrit* (the tablets of the covenant), forty days later, on Yom Kippur. That period, during which the people begged for forgiveness and Moses pleaded for the people, was the first instance of the Jews performing *teshuvah* on a national level. The fact that we were given a second chance, and received the Ten Commandments, was in the merit of that *teshuvah*. Since then, the period between Rosh Chodesh Elul and Yom Kippur has been a fixed time for repentance and forgiveness for every generation — our chance to make it right between God and us, again and again.

In the Torah, Elul is only referred to as the sixth month. At the time that the month names were adopted, the Jews spoke Aramaic; and in Aramaic, the word 'Elul' means 'search' — a perfect name for a month during which we search our hearts.

Elul is a time when we engage in a daily *cheshbon nefesh*: a spiritual accounting. We attempt to acknowledge all of our mistakes, misdeeds and miscommunications over the course of the year, and to assess the character traits and behavioral patterns that have led to these negative elements in our lives. The imperfections and shortcomings that we have illuminated through our *cheshbon hanefesh* must be addressed. Elul is the time for cleaning our slates. First, we focus on our human interactions, and fix whatever is in our power to fix, even if all we can do is apologize to an injured party. Only once we have achieved wholeness in our human relationships can we ask God for forgiveness, and hope to increase our spiritual connection to Him. Toward the end of the month, as the moon wanes and its light dims, we prepare for our encounter with the New Year.

Psalm 27

א לְדָוִד ה׳ אוֹרִי וְיִשְׁעִי מִמִּי אִירָא ה׳ מָעוֹז
חַיַּי מִמִּי אֶפְחָד: ב בִּקְרֹב עָלַי מְרֵעִים לֶאֱכֹל
אֶת־בְּשָׂרִי צָרַי וְאֹיְבַי לִי הֵמָּה כָּשְׁלוּ וְנָפָלוּ: ג
אִם־תַּחֲנֶה עָלַי מַחֲנֶה לֹא־יִירָא לִבִּי אִם־תָּקוּם
עָלַי מִלְחָמָה בְּזֹאת אֲנִי בוֹטֵחַ: ד אַחַת שָׁאַלְתִּי
מֵאֵת־ה׳ אוֹתָהּ אֲבַקֵּשׁ שִׁבְתִּי בְּבֵית־ה׳ כָּל־
יְמֵי חַיַּי לַחֲזוֹת בְּנֹעַם־ה׳ וּלְבַקֵּר בְּהֵיכָלוֹ: ה כִּי
יִצְפְּנֵנִי (בְּסֻכֹּה) [בְּסֻכּוֹ] בְּיוֹם רָעָה יַסְתִּירֵנִי
בְּסֵתֶר אָהֳלוֹ בְּצוּר יְרוֹמְמֵנִי: ו וְעַתָּה יָרוּם רֹאשִׁי
עַל־אֹיְבַי סְבִיבוֹתַי וְאֶזְבְּחָה בְאָהֳלוֹ זִבְחֵי תְרוּעָה
אָשִׁירָה וַאֲזַמְּרָה לַיהֹוָ־ה: ז שְׁמַע־ה׳ קוֹלִי
אֶקְרָא וְחָנֵּנִי וַעֲנֵנִי: ח לְךָ אָמַר לִבִּי בַּקְּשׁוּ פָנָי
אֶת־פָּנֶיךָ ה׳ אֲבַקֵּשׁ: ט אַל־תַּסְתֵּר פָּנֶיךָ מִמֶּנִּי
אַל־תַּט בְּאַף עַבְדֶּךָ עֶזְרָתִי הָיִיתָ אַל־תִּטְּשֵׁנִי
וְאַל־תַּעַזְבֵנִי אֱלֹהֵי יִשְׁעִי: י כִּי־אָבִי וְאִמִּי עֲזָבוּנִי
וַיהֹוָ־ה יַאַסְפֵנִי: יא הוֹרֵנִי ה׳ דַּרְכֶּךָ וּנְחֵנִי בְּאֹרַח
מִישׁוֹר לְמַעַן שׁוֹרְרָי: יב אַל־תִּתְּנֵנִי בְּנֶפֶשׁ
צָרָי כִּי קָמוּ־בִי עֵדֵי־שֶׁקֶר וִיפֵחַ חָמָס: יג לוּלֵא

הֶאֱמַנְתִּי לִרְאוֹת בְּטוּב־ה׳ בְּאֶרֶץ חַיִּים: יד קַוֵּה
אֶל־ה׳ חֲזַק וְיַאֲמֵץ לִבֶּךָ וְקַוֵּה אֶל־ה׳

A Psalm of David. God is my light and my salvation; whom shall I fear? The Lord is the stronghold of my life; of whom shall I be afraid?

When evildoers assail me, uttering slanders against me, my adversaries and foes, they shall stumble and fall.

Though a host encamp against me, my heart shall not fear; though war arise against me, yet I will be confident.

One thing I ask of God, one thing I request: To dwell in the house of God all the days of my life To behold God's graciousness, and to visit in His palace.

For he will hide me in his shelter in the day of trouble; he will conceal me under the cover of his tent, he will set me high upon a rock.

And now my head shall be lifted up above my enemies round about me; and I will offer in His tent sacrifices, with shouts of joy; I will sing and make melody to God.

Hear, O God, when I cry aloud, be gracious to me and answer me! Thou hast said, "Seek ye my face." My heart says to thee, "Thy face, God, do I seek."

Hide not thy face from me. Turn not thy servant away in anger, thou who hast been my help. Cast me not off, forsake me not, God of my salvation!

For my father and my mother have forsaken me, but God will take me up.

Teach me thy way, God; and lead me on a level path because of my enemies.

Give me not up to the will of my adversaries; for false witnesses have risen against me, and they breathe out violence.

I believe that I shall see the goodness of God in the land of the living!

Wait for God; be strong, and let your heart take courage; yea, hope for God!

Relating this psalm to *teshuvah*, we could well understand it as a plea for help in dealing with the enemy within; with whatever tendencies or weaknesses we identify during our *cheshbon nefesh* that we know we must battle, as they work against the development of our deepest, truest selves. Elul is the time to ask God to help you rise above your undesirable traits, since He is with you in the *field* and more attainable. Go out to meet Him — in your home, your workplace and your community — turn them into dwelling places for God by sanctifying each of these places with the performance of *mitzvot* in any way that you can.

Reflective Questions

1. Share your insights into Psalm 27.

2. What would it be like if you could join God for that walk in the field? What would you share about your life? What would you ask for?

3. In what way will you seek to restore your personal relationship with God this month?

4. Do you believe that self-transformation is truly possible? Do you want to change? Are you prepared to try your best to do so?

5. Identify and describe one damaging pattern that you want to break in the coming year. List one thing you must do in order to break that pattern.

Take home thoughts: According to Jewish tradition, God cannot forgive us for sins committed against another person until we have first obtained forgiveness from the person we have wronged. Do an inventory check of all the people you think you might have wronged and find it in your heart to ask them for forgiveness by writing, calling or visiting them.

Kavanah for Hafrashat Challah

Our transgressions and sins create a separation between us and God. We alone know what is in our hearts and what our sins are. We know which areas require improvement, which character traits need to be refined. Ask God to help you overcome your flawed character traits. Pray that the performance of the *Hafrashat Challah* will bring you a step higher to the source of holiness, so that he may hear your plea.

The procedure and blessing for the *hafrashat challah* ceremony can be found on pages 14-17. Participants may wish to shape the challah afterwards, or take it home and shape it there.

ADDITIONAL CHALLAH RECIPES

Here you will find basic recipes as well as healthier alternatives such as Whole-Wheat Challah and Gluten-Free Oat Challah. Traditionally, challah loaves are sprinkled with sesame or poppy seeds to recall the manna, the "bread from heaven," that glittered like jewels in the early morning sun. The Torah describes the manna as plentiful, and looking like coriander seeds (Numbers 11:7), so we sprinkle seeds on the challah to recall that divine bounty.

You will notice that most of the ingredients listed are organic, because I believe that every detail is important in the creation of challah, starting from how the ingredients it is made from are grown. We honor the ancient roots of Judaism, within which agriculture and religion were intertwined, tying up the most fundamental elements of life with a vision of the divine.

In order to be able to fulfill the *mitzvah* of *hafrashat challah*, each recipe uses 5 pounds (2.25 kg) of flour.

Helpful Tips

In most recipes through out this book, more than 4 cups of warm water is called for in the ingredient list. Making challah is not an exact science, and there are times due to humidity in the air, temperature and altitude where more or less water is required. If your dough is too dry after integrating all the ingredients with the flour, add increments of ¼ cup (60 ml) warm water to the flour until the desired consistency is reached. Conversely, if your dough is too wet, and sticking to the bowl or your fingers, then add ¼ cup (30 g) increments of flour until the dough is no longer sticky.

Dry yeast is widely available and sold in large packets. After the first use, seal and store in a glass jar in the freezer. If you purchase the *active* dry yeast in strips of three ¼ oz. (7g) packets, you will need 4 packets of active dry yeast for every 5 pounds (2.25 kg) of flour. When using dry yeast from the refrigerator or freezer, it's best to bring it to room temperature before using. The main advantage of using dry yeast is that it can be stored in the freezer for up to 6 months.

Yeast needs to multiply and grow in warm water and sugar; this is known as as *proofing*. After 10 minutes, the yeast should begin to form a creamy foam on the surface of the water. You can now proceed to combine the yeast mixture with the flour and other dry ingredients. If there is no foam in the bowl, the yeast is dead and you should start over with a new batch of yeast.

Egg Challah

You will notice that most of the recipes throughout the book are water challahs, because that is the more traditional recipe for challah. The addition of eggs in challah was a tradition of Ashkenazi Jews from Eastern Europe.

Yields: 8 medium challahs

Ingredients

4 tablespoons active dry yeast

3 cups (700 ml) warm water

¾ cup (150 g) organic sugar plus 2 tablespoons organic sugar

4 cage-free organic eggs

5 pounds (2.25 kg) organic white flour

1 ½ tablespoons sea salt

1 cup (230 ml) neutral-tasting oil, such as safflower oil

Topping

2 cage-free organic eggs, beaten

1 In a large bowl, combine the yeast with the 2 tablespoons of sugar and the warm water. Cover the bowl and allow the mixture to start activating. Yeast activation should take about 10 minutes; it will be bubbling and foamy.

2 In the meantime, break 1 egg at a time into a small glass bowl and check that there are no red spots on the yolk. Transfer the egg into a larger bowl and, when all the eggs are cracked, beat with a fork.

3 Set 1 cup (125 g) of flour aside. Sift the remaining flour, sugar and salt into the bowl.

4 Pour the eggs and oil onto the flour. Combine all the ingredients, using a spatula. When it begins to form a dough, it is time to knead. At this point, you can remove the dough from the bowl and knead on the kitchen counter if it's easier for you, or knead directly in the bowl.

5 To knead the dough: grab the side of the dough furthest away from you and fold it toward yourself. Fold the dough in half and use your body weight to push the dough into itself. If you find that the dough is sticking too much to the surface and preventing you from kneading properly, dust the dough with flour. Give the dough a quarter turn (90 degrees). Grab the other side and fold it in half. Again, with a lot of weight behind it, push the newly folded half into itself. Repeat this process for 10-15 minutes, or until the dough is smooth, silky, elastic and it does not stick to the surface.

6   After the dough is thoroughly prepared, lay it on the countertop while you grease the bowl with a fine layer of oil. Next, turn the dough in the oil several times so that the dough is greased lightly on all sides.

7   Cover the bowl with a large plastic garbage bag or kitchen towel and allow it to rise for 1 hour.

8   Make the blessing on *hafrashat challah* — see **Hafrashat Challah, page 17.**

9   Knead the dough again for a few more minutes. Use the remaining flour for the surface area and hands to prevent sticking. Form it into shaped loaves of your choice.

10   Cover the loaves again and let them rise in a warm place for 1 hour or until the dough has doubled in volume from its original size.

11   If you cannot bake the challahs immediately, then this is the time to wrap the shaped dough in plastic wrap to prevent drying. You can store it in the coldest part of the refrigerator for up to 48 hours. On the day of baking, remove the dough from refrigerator and let stand on kitchen counter until it comes to room temperature, about one hour.

12   Preheat the oven to 350° F (180° C). Brush your challahs with beaten eggs and sprinkle with the topping of your choice (traditional choices are sesame seeds or poppy seeds).

13   Bake in your preheated oven for about 30-35 minutes, or until loaves turn golden brown and shiny. Bread should have a nice hollow sound when thumped on the bottom.

14   Remove from the oven and cool on a rack. Wait at least one hour before serving. If you are freezing the challah, wrap in waxed paper and foil. It can be stored in the freezer for up to 2 months.

Basic Challah
using Fresh Yeast

Fresh yeast is harder to come by than dry yeast. It is found in the refrigerated section of the supermarket and should be kept in the refrigerator until ready to use. If you have difficulty finding fresh yeast, you can try your local kosher bakery and ask them if they stock it. Often they do — it's a little known secret.

Yields: 8 medium challahs

Ingredients

1 ½ cubes or 3 ounces (90 g) fresh yeast

4 ½ cups (1.1 liters) warm water

¾ cup (150 g) organic sugar plus 2 tablespoons organic sugar

5 pounds (2.25 kg) organic white flour

1 ½ tablespoons sea salt

1 cup (230 ml) neutral-tasting oil, such as safflower oil

Topping

2 cage-free organic eggs, beaten

1 In a large bowl, combine the yeast with the 2 tablespoons of sugar and the warm water. Cover the bowl and allow the mixture to start activating. Yeast activation should take about 10 minutes; it will be bubbling and foamy.

2 Set 1 cup (125 g) of flour aside. Sift the remaining flour, sugar and salt into the bowl.

3 Pour the oil onto the flour. Combine all the ingredients, using a spatula. When it begins to form a dough, it is time to knead. At this point, you can remove the dough from the bowl and knead on the kitchen counter if it's easier for you, or directly in the bowl.

4 To knead the dough: grab the side of the dough furthest away from you and fold it toward yourself. Fold the dough in half and use your body weight to push the dough into itself. If you find that the dough is sticking too much to the surface and preventing you from kneading properly, dust the dough with flour. Give the dough a quarter turn (90 degrees). Grab the other side and fold it in half. Again, with a lot of weight behind it, push the newly folded half into itself. Repeat this process for 10-15 minutes or until the dough is smooth, silky, elastic and it does not stick to the surface.

5 After the dough is thoroughly prepared, lay it on the countertop while you grease the bowl with a fine layer of oil. Next, turn the dough in the oil several times so that the dough is greased lightly on all sides.

6 Cover the bowl with a large plastic garbage bag or kitchen towel and allow it to rise for 1 hour.

7 Make the blessing on *hafrashat challah* — see ***Hafrashat Challah, page 17***

8 Knead the dough again for a few more minutes. Use the remaining cup of flour for the surface area and hands to prevent sticking. Form it into shaped loaves of your choice.

9 Cover the loaves again and let them rise in a warm place for 1 hour, or until the dough has doubled in volume from its original size.

10 If you cannot bake the challahs immediately, then this is the time to wrap the shaped dough in plastic wrap to prevent drying. You can store it in the coldest part of the refrigerator for up to 48 hours. On the day of baking, remove the dough from the refrigerator and let stand on kitchen counter until it comes to room temperature, about one hour.

11 Preheat the oven to 350° F (180° C). Brush your challahs with beaten eggs and sprinkle with the topping of your choice (traditional choices are sesame seeds or poppy seeds).

12 Bake in your preheated oven for about 30-35 minutes, or until loaves turn golden brown and shiny. Bread should have a nice hollow sound when thumped on the bottom.

13 Remove from the oven and cool on a rack. Wait at least one hour before serving. If you are freezing the challah, wrap in waxed paper and foil. It can be stored in the freezer for up to 2 months.

Spelt Challah

Spelt flour can work as an alternative to those with a wheat sensitivity, since it is low in gluten. If you are short on time, this challah takes the least amount of time of all the recipes in this book, as it does not require the same amount of kneading or rising. Since it is a light challah, eggs are usually omitted, making it a wonderful option for vegans. It has a tendency to unfold, so placing the dough in a baking pan after you have shaped it will ensure it holds its shape during baking.

Yields: 8 medium challahs

Ingredients

2 ½ tablespoons active dry yeast

5 cups (1.2 liters) warm water

1 cup (200 g) organic sugar plus 2 tablespoons organic sugar

5 pounds (2.25 kg) organic spelt flour

1 ½ tablespoons sea salt

1 cup (230 ml) neutral-tasting oil, such as safflower oil

Topping

¼ cup (60 ml) Soy Milk or Almond Milk, for washing

1 In a large bowl, combine the yeast with the 2 tablespoons of sugar and the warm water. Cover the bowl and allow the mixture to start activating. Yeast activation should take about 10 minutes; it will be bubbling and foamy.

2 Set 1 cup (125 g) of flour aside. Sift the remaining flour, sugar and salt into the bowl.

3 Pour the oil onto the flour. Combine all the ingredients, using a spatula. When it begins to form a dough, it is time to knead. At this point, you can remove the dough from the bowl and knead on the kitchen counter if it's easier for you, or knead directly in the bowl.

4 To knead the dough: grab the side of the dough furthest away from you and fold it toward yourself. Fold the dough in half and use your body weight to push the dough into itself. If you find that the dough is sticking too much to the surface and preventing you from kneading properly, dust the dough with flour. Give the dough a quarter turn (90 degrees). Grab the other side and fold it in half. Again, with a lot of weight behind it, push the newly folded half into itself. Repeat this process for 7 minutes, or until the dough is smooth, silky, elastic and it does not stick to the surface.

5 After the dough is thoroughly prepared, lay it on the countertop while you grease the bowl with a fine layer of oil. Next, turn the dough in the oil several times so that the dough is greased lightly on all sides.

6 Cover the bowl with a large plastic garbage bag or kitchen towel and allow it to rise for 35 minutes.

7 Make the blessing on *hafrashat challah* — see **Hafrashat Challah, page 17**

8 Knead the dough again for a few more minutes. Use the remaining flour for the surface area and hands to prevent sticking.

9 If you plan on cooking it the same day, form it into shaped loaves of your choice and place in baking pans. (If not, then this is the time to wrap the dough in plastic wrap to prevent drying. You can store it in the coldest part of the refrigerator for up to 48 hours. On the day of baking, remove the dough from refrigerator and let stand on kitchen counter until it comes to room temperature, about one hour. Shape into loaves and place in baking pans).

10 Cover again and let the loaves rise in a warm place for 35 minutes or until the dough has doubled in volume from its original size.

11 Preheat the oven to 350° F (180° C). Brush your challahs with soymilk or almond milk and sprinkle with the topping of your choice (traditional choices are sesame seeds or poppy seeds).

12 Bake in your preheated oven for about 30-35 minutes, or until loaves turn golden brown and shiny. Bread should have a nice hollow sound when thumped on the bottom.

13 Remove from the oven and cool on a rack. Wait at least one hour before serving. If you are freezing the challah, wrap in waxed paper and foil. It can be stored in the freezer for up to 2 months.

Whole-Wheat Challah

Whole-wheat flour has a tendency to become rancid faster than white flour, so it's best to buy it from a store with a high turnover, or directly from a mill. Whole-wheat challah requires more patience than white flour, as it needs more time to rise, so keep that in mind when starting this recipe.

Yields: 8 medium challahs

Ingredients

4 tablespoons active dry yeast

5 ½ cups (1.3 liter) warm water

1 ½ cup (300 g) organic packed brown sugar plus 2 tablespoons organic sugar

5 pounds (2.25 kg) organic whole-wheat flour

1 ½ tablespoons sea salt

1 cup (230 ml) neutral-tasting oil, such as safflower oil

Topping

2 cage-free organic eggs, beaten

Seeds, for sprinkling

1. In a large bowl, combine the yeast with the 2 tablespoons of sugar and the warm water. Cover the bowl and allow the mixture to start activating. Yeast activation should take about 10 minutes; it will be bubbling and foamy.

2. Set 1 cup (125 g) of flour aside. Sift the remaining flour, sugar and salt into the bowl.

3. Pour the oil onto the flour. Combine all the ingredients, using a spatula. When it begins to form a dough, it is time to knead. At this point, you can remove the dough from the bowl and knead on the kitchen counter if it's easier for you, or knead directly in the bowl.

4. To knead the dough: grab the side of the dough furthest away from you and fold it toward yourself. Fold the dough in half and use your body weight to push the dough into itself. If you find that the dough is sticking too much to the surface and preventing you from kneading properly, dust the dough with flour. Give the dough a quarter turn (90 degrees). Grab the other side and fold it in half. Again, with a lot of weight behind it, push the newly folded half into itself. Repeat this process for 10-15 minutes, or until the dough is smooth, silky, elastic and it does not stick to the surface. **If the dough is too difficult to knead and you are struggling with it, let the dough rest for 30 minutes, and then return to kneading.**

5. After the dough is thoroughly prepared, lay it on the countertop while you grease the bowl with a fine layer of oil. Next, turn the dough in the oil several times so that the dough is greased lightly on all sides.

6   Cover the bowl with a large plastic garbage bag or kitchen towel and allow it to rise for **1 ½ hours**.

7   Make the blessing on *hafrashat challah* — see **Hafrashat Challah, page 17**

8   Knead the dough again for a few more minutes. Use the remaining flour for the surface area and hands to prevent sticking. Form it into shaped loaves of your choice.

9   Cover the loaves again and let them rise in a warm place for 1 hour or until the dough has doubled in volume from its original size.

10 If you cannot bake the challahs immediately, then this is the time to wrap the shaped dough in plastic wrap to prevent drying. You can store it in the coldest part of the refrigerator for up to 48 hours. On the day of baking, remove the dough from refrigerator and let stand on kitchen counter until it comes to room temperature, about one hour.

11 Preheat the oven to 350° F (180° C). Brush your challahs with beaten eggs and sprinkle with the topping of your choice.

12 Bake in your preheated oven for about 30-35 minutes, or until loaves turn golden brown and shiny. Bread should have a nice hollow sound when thumped on the bottom.

13 Remove from the oven and cool on a rack. Wait at least one hour before serving. If you are freezing the challah, wrap in waxed paper and foil. It can be stored in the freezer for up to 2 months.

Gluten-Free Oat Challah

Gluten-free dough is on the wet side and needs to be put in a mold to hold its shape. It cannot be braided. You can purchase a challah-shaped mold or pour batter into a muffin pan for mini rolls. This challah is wonderful for those gluten-free folks who would like to have challah that can be used on Shabbat with the *hamotzi* blessing over bread. Since the amount of oat flour in this recipe is small, you should perform *hafrashat challah,* although **without** a blessing. If you have a question about saying *hamotzi* on this challah, you should consult your Rabbi.

Yields: 8 – 12 muffins

Ingredients

1 tablespoon active dry yeast

¼ cup (50 g) brown sugar plus 1 tablespoon organic sugar

1 cup (235 ml) warm water

3 cage-free organic eggs

¼ cup (60 ml) neutral-tasting oil, such as safflower oil

1 teaspoon apple cider vinegar

1 ½ cups (240 g) certified gluten-free oat flour

½ cup (70 g) sweet rice flour

¼ cup (35 g) sorghum flour

¼ cup (30 g) tapioca flour

1 tablespoon ground flax seeds

1 teaspoon salt

1 In a large bowl, combine the yeast with the 2 tablespoons of sugar and the warm water. Cover the bowl and allow the mixture to start activating. Yeast activation should take about 10 minutes; it will be bubbling and foamy.

2 In the meantime, break 1 egg at a time into a small glass bowl and check that there are no red spots on the yolk. Transfer the egg into a larger bowl and, when all the eggs are cracked, beat with a fork.

3 Combine eggs, oil and vinegar and pour into yeast mixture.

4 Combine dry ingredients with the yeast mixture in the bowl. Mix for 10-15 minutes. The dough will be on the wet side, but should hold together.

5 Place the batter into a mold of your choice, either muffin pan or a challah mold.

6 Let rise 1 ½ — 2 hours. Preheat the oven to 350° F (180° C).

7 Bake in your preheated oven for about 20-25 minutes, or until muffins turn golden brown.

ADDITIONAL CHALLAH SHAPES

It has been traditional for many centuries that the challahs we eat on Shabbat are braided loaves. This is only tradition, not law, which is why we can choose to use other shapes to honor some of the themes of the Jewish year.

There are various ideas put forth as to why we eat braided loaves, beyond the fact that they simply look more fancy than regular bread. One common idea is that the braids are supposed to add up to twelve, to represent the twelve show breads that were placed on a table in the Temple every week. So, for example, if you use four challahs of three braids each, two per meal, then you reach twelve. Or if you use two loaves with six braids each at each meal, then you reach twelve at each meal (as opposed to over the whole Shabbat).

One idea suggests that the three-braided challah represents the commandment to observe Shabbat. In Exodus, God commands the people to "remember" (*zachor*) the Sabbath day, because "in six days God created the heavens and earth and on the seventh day he rested" (Exodus 20: 8, 11). In Deuteronomy, God commands the people to "guard" (*shamor*) the Sabbath day because they "were slaves in Egypt, and God brought you out with a strong hand and an outstretched arm" (Deuteronomy 5: 12, 15). One braid is for the command to remember, and the second is for the command to guard. According to a tradition given in the Gemara, God actually spoke these two different words, two different aspects of the same command, in the same breath, "*bedibur echad*" — and the third braid represents that fact; that God said them simultaneously and as one unit.

There is a tradition in the Talmud that God Himself braided Eve's hair in preparation for her wedding to Adam, as His wedding gift to the couple (*Brachot* 61a). I like to understand this as God arranging Eve's creative energies, channeling her imagination into an ordered form that would allow her to maximize her potential as a wife.

For me, within a Rosh Chodesh group, braiding challah represents the idea of unity: the different strands represent the diversity of the participants; unique individuals tied together into the peaceful harmony of Shabbat. Sometimes, when I braid alone, I think of the strands as representing my thoughts, the days of the week, the conversations I've had, all pulled together into the challah as a cohesive form.

As we braid these challahs, in addition to the more traditional meaning behind the braids, we can focus on these ideas; we can think of God plaiting Eve's hair and channeling her energy, and think of ourselves focusing and giving positive order to the energies of our homes.

Single-Strand Challah

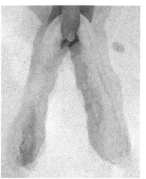

1   Roll out a ball of dough into a long strand (you can make the strand shorter to make a mini challah).

2   With your index finger and thumb, pick up the rope from the center. It will look like two strands. Your fingers will work as a placeholder for the loop.

3   Working from the top, twist the strands around each other, until you reach the bottom.

4   Pinch the ends together and slip the end into the hole that was created where you originally picked up the strand.

Two-Strand Challah

1 Divide each piece of dough into two equal parts. Roll into two even strands.

2 Place one strand on top of the other, like a cross. Bring south to north and north to south, with south passing to the left of north as they cross.

3 Bring east to west and west to east, with east passing above west as they cross.

4 Repeat this process until all the dough is used. Press the remaining ends together. There should be a distinct taper, creating a teardrop shape.

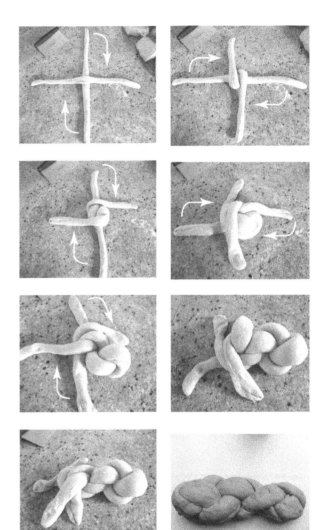

Four-Strand Challah

1   Divide each piece of dough into 4 equal parts to form the braid. Roll out the dough into even and uniform strands.

2   Lay the strands side by side, separating each strand, and pinch together at the top.

3   Pick up the outer left strand and the outer right strand, and cross them over (forming an X) into the center, between strand 2 and strand 3.

4   Strand 2 and strand 3 will now be on the outer ends. Again, pick up the outer left strand and the outer right strand and cross them over into the center.

5   Continue working from the outer strands. When there are no more strands, pinch together at the end and tuck them in for a clean finish.

Six-Strand Challah

1. Divide each piece of dough into 6 equal parts to form the braid. Roll out the dough into even and uniform strands.

2. Place 2 strands on the surface area, parallel to each other, leaving some room between each other for another strand. Place 3 strands, perpendicular to the 2 strands, forming a cross.

3. Place the last strand on top of the 3 strands. It is the only strand that is over the 3 strands.

4. Braid all four corners, and pinch closed at the ends.

5. Take the top strand, and slide it over to the second braid, pinching them closed. Do the same with the remaining two braids.

Spiral Challah — Festivals

The round challah symbolizes the continuity and cyclicality of life and is typically eaten on Rosh Hashana and other festivals.

1   Roll out a piece of dough of dough into a long strand.

2   If you are using a filling (such as apple), add a thin line at the center of the flattened dough going all the way down until 2 inches (5 cm) from the ends.

3   Roll the strand till it becomes smooth, using gentle pressure with your hands on the center of the strand, pulling outward as you roll. Pinch the ends together. Re-flour the surface as needed to keep your dough from sticking. Starting from the tapered end, swirl the dough into a spiral.

Pictures can be found in the chapter **Tishrei,** *pages 35-38.*

Spiritual Kneading through the Jewish Months covers all twelve months of the Jewish year, along with the extra Adar in a Jewish Leap year. After a *Spiritual Kneading* group has completed a full year of Rosh Chodesh meetings, they can consult this list if they wish to develop another course of study for the following year.

The fullest understanding of our festivals is attained from experiencing them firsthand, but reading about their history and purpose is vital for a true appreciation. The books suggested below are those I found helpful in my own study, and in writing this book.

Seasons of Our Joy: A Modern Guide to the Jewish Holidays by Arthur Waskow

From Rosh Hashanah to Tisha B'Av, this guide provides rituals, recipes, songs, prayers and suggestions for new approaches to holiday observance. The book explores the meaning of each holiday in relation to the history of the Jewish people, and suggests rituals and spiritual practices to follow in preparation for each festival.

The Book of Our Heritage [Box set] by Eliyahu Ki Tov

A beloved classic that explores festivals and fast days and explains their laws and customs. Midrashic commentaries and insights by great Jewish thinkers and spiritual leaders enhance the inspiring text.

Jewish Meditation: A Practical Guide by Aryeh Kaplan

This book is a must for any Jewish individual seeking spirituality. It was the first Jewish text I read as I was becoming a serious student. It left an indelible imprint, and was part of the motivation behind the writing of this book. It offers a step-by-step introduction to meditation, and the Jewish practice of meditation in particular. It is a practical guide that covers such topics as mantra meditation, contemplation and visualization within a Jewish context. It explains how to use meditative techniques to enhance prayer. Through simple exercises and clear explanations of theory, Rabbi Kaplan presents the tools to develop spiritual potential through an authentically Jewish meditative practice.

The Hallah Book: Recipes, History, and Traditions by Freda Reider

The author describes twenty-one different challah shapes, and their associations with different holidays.

The Rosh Hodesh Table: Foods at the New Moon by Judith Y. Solomon

A sweet little book on Jewish food lore. Includes biblical and historical food references and recipes related to each month.

The Commentators' Rosh Chodesh: Halachic and Aggadic Interpretation, Laws and Customs Regarding the Celebration of the New Month by Yitzchak Sender

An in-depth book on the history of Rosh Chodesh and the surrounding customs and laws that provides a deep appreciation and understanding of the Jewish months.

The Encyclopedia of Jewish Symbols by Ellen Frankel and Betsy Patkin Teutsch

This book is helpful in explaining Jewish ceremonial objects and images, personalities, places, concepts, motifs and events that continue to play a meaningful role in defining Jewish experience today.

The Midrash Says: The Narrative of the Weekly Torah-portion in the Perspective of Our Sages (Five Vol. Set) by Moshe Weissman

A selection of the most well-known midrashic stories based on the weekly Torah portion, taken from Talmud and Midrash. This popular series will not fail to inspire and stimulate the reader, while providing fascinating supplementary information on the weekly portion.

Women at the Crossroads: A Woman's Perspective on the Weekly Torah Portion by Chana Bracha Siegelbaum

A very accessible, easy-to-understand book that comprises fifty-three essays, one for each of the weekly Torah portions. The author explores the underlying values of laws and rituals that pertain to women by examining the inherent nature of women as presented in the Torah. Based on the intricacies of the Torah text, she shows the beauty and depth of the role of women as portrayed in the Torah, examines the dilemmas the women of the Torah faced and teaches the importance of women and their immense influence on society as prime movers of history.

WITH GRATITUDE...

Long before I was conducting Rosh Chodesh groups in my home, I was introduced to challah baking by my friend, Brenda Sassoon-Rozmarin. She invited me to her home on a Thursday night to participate in a *Segula* Challah bake (see more on that, page 26). It was my very first time baking challah. It was touching, I thought, that Brenda and I were part of the forty women from around the community, baking in our own homes — all connecting to a shared intention. There was something very holy and meditative about the whole process. In a sense, I felt like I was part of the pulse of the Jewish heartbeat.

The next day, I adorned my Shabbat table with these fresh, homemade challahs, covered with a very colorful African-inspired challah cover — an ode to my South African husband's roots. My husband, Mervin, oohed and aahed with every bite. His appreciation, combined with the experience of the *cegulah* challah bake, inspired me to begin trying to bake challah for Shabbat regularly.

At that time, I was also participating in a women's meditation group, which is where I met a brilliant Torah scholar, Jocelyn. It was during one of our discussions that Jocelyn told me that gatherings of women were an inherent part of Judaism. She told me about Rosh Chodesh and how it was a woman's holiday, and that was when my idea of creating a Rosh Chodesh Challah Baking group came to me. When I shared my idea with Jocelyn, she excitedly pointed me to numerous Torah references on challah. I discovered that there is even an entire tractate in the Mishna called *Challah*. Through serious study, I found ways to connect baking challah with a relevant theme of each Jewish month.

Jocelyn recommended that I sign up with Partners in Torah, which is how Chaya Sara Stark came into my life like a breath of fresh air. Chaya Sara and I developed a special connection right away, when we discovered our shared reverence for the late Rabbi Aryeh Kaplan. Chaya Sara was a student of his. When this manuscript was ready (or so I thought), it was Chaya Sara who read every word and gently, very gently, gave me her feedback. There was a lot of work to do, she said, but she was always on the sideline cheering me on, emphatic that this book *needed* to be published.

Once the book was fleshed out, God simply knocked me on the head with Deborah Meghnagi Bailey, my editor, who pushed, pulled, stretched, punched and knocked me down like a challah in her hands, only to rebuild this manuscript into the gem that it is. She took my glob of dough (so to speak) and helped shape it with her very precise and thoughtful feedback. Along the way, I became a better Torah student, because of the research this book entailed.

I am grateful to those women who attended the *Spiritual Kneading* group, asking questions that furthered my studies. The truth is that, starting out, I knew virtually nothing on the topics of challah and Rosh Chodesh; I formed the Rosh Chodesh group because *I* wanted to learn more. I became the teacher and the perpetual student.

165

Thank you, Alisa Roberts, my proofreader, whose ability to detect the minutest typos is mind-boggling.

Thank you, Joanna Dion Brown, who designed my vision for this book. We met at the artistic celestial plane and just created from there. Much gratitude for your patience and enthusiasm in striving to perfect the look of this book.

Thank you, Jonah, my son. Jonah blessed the *Spiritual Kneading* group with the *birkat hakohanim* (priestly benediction) during the challah baking process. What a tremendous *zechut* (merit) we had to be blessed by a descendent of the very *kohanim* we would have tithed our *challah* to during Temple times. I hope that one day, you will find that woman of valor who will appreciate your warm heart with her own fresh-baked challahs, light your home with Shabbat candles and always keep your family sacred.

A deep thank you to my husband, Mervin, who gladly gave me the space to learn and write. You have encouraged me to explore the feminine divine within. I thank you for the safety and security you have provided me with so that I could cultivate my femininity.

Finally, I want to thank God for gracing me with the idea of this book. I believe that the only reason I was able to see this book through was because God was holding my hand throughout the entire process, sending me the words, knowledge and people who helped me compile it. I felt Him up close, always encouraging me to learn, write and teach. *This* is my challah!

ABOUT THE AUTHOR

Dahlia Abraham-Klein holds a Master's of Science in Education. She has been conducting *Spiritual Kneading* Rosh Chodesh Challah Baking groups within her Long Island community since 2010. She has taught privately in her home, as well as to larger groups in local synagogues and Adult Learning centers. She has previously published a cookbook, *Silk Road Vegetarian: Vegan, Vegetarian and Gluten Free Recipes for the Mindful Cook* (Tuttle 2014). The cookbook focuses on Dahlia's ancestral Jewish cuisine from Central Asia, and includes over one hundred gluten-free recipes that utilize local ingredients, making the dishes more accessible to the West. Dahlia Abraham-Klein can be found at: www.silkroadvegetarian.com.